Euripides

## The Ion of Euripides

Now First Translated into English, in its Original Metres, and Supplied...

Euripides

**The Ion of Euripides**
*Now First Translated into English, in its Original Metres, and Supplied...*

ISBN/EAN: 9783337139896

Printed in Europe, USA, Canada, Australia, Japan

Cover: Foto ©Thomas Meinert / pixelio.de

More available books at **www.hansebooks.com**

THE

# ION

OF

# EURIPIDES,

NOW FIRST TRANSLATED INTO ENGLISH,

IN ITS ORIGINAL METRES,

AND SUPPLIED WITH STAGE DIRECTIONS

SUGGESTING HOW IT MAY HAVE BEEN

PERFORMED ON THE ATHENIAN STAGE,

WITH PREFACE AND NOTES,

BY

## H. B. L.

"NIL PURIS, SANCTISQUE ANIMIS SPERARE NEGATUR;
NULLA MALIS CERTA EST SORS TIBI DICIT ION."—*Barnes.*

WILLIAMS AND NORGATE,
14, HENRIETTA STREET, COVENT GARDEN, LONDON;
AND 20, SOUTH FREDERICK STREET, EDINBURGH.
1889.

LONDON :

G. NORMAN AND SON, PRINTERS, HART STREET,

COVENT GARDEN.

# CONTENTS.

# PREFACE.

" Die Flamme freilich ist verschwunden,
    doch ist mir um die Welt nicht Leid ;
    hier bleibt genug Poeten einzuweihen
    zu stiften Gild und Handswerksneid,
    und kann ich die Talenten nicht verleihen,
    verborg ich wenigstens das Kleid."
            *Göthe. Faust. Theil. 2. Akt 3.*

" Rhyme is no necessary adjunct of poem or good verse, but the invention of a barbarous age to set off wretched matter and lame metre . . . . Italian and Spanish poets, of prime note, have rejected rhyme both in longer and shorter works, as have, long since, our best English tragedy writers, as a thing of itself to all judicious ears trivial and of no musical delight . . . . . . avoided by the learned ancients both in poetry and good oratory."
            *Milton's Preface to Paradise Lost.*

BOTH the Iambic and Trochaic metres are employed in the dialogues of this play, and various forms of the Lyric in its odes. This piece is written in 1048 Iambic, 84 Trochaic, and 490 Lyric lines.

The Iambic trimeter acatalectic of the Greek drama, approaching, according to the judgment of Aristotle, nearest to common discourse, which, for a long time, was popular amongst the Latins, appears to have been entirely disused by their reprentatives in modern Italy, for their only twelve syllable-lined metre, the *sdrucciolo*, is not Iambic ; the beat, in Italian verses, never occurs upon their ultimate.

In France a metre resembling the Iambic in some respects, the Senarian, better known as the Alexandrine, so called from the poem *Alexandre* written in the thirteenth century, from that period until the present time has been, invariably, used in all heroic and serious dramatic verse.

In England, if we except Browning's *Fifine at the fair*, 1872, and a few quite recent imitations from the Greek Iambic, it would be difficult to find an entire poem written in it, although, in the works of ancient and modern poets special and incidental lines of Senarian have been frequently introduced.

In Germany it is seldom met with. Göthe has availed himself of it in his *Klassisches Walpurgis Nacht*, as also, lately, have translators of Greek plays and the poets of the *Kladderadatsch*.

In the Netherlands it is to be found in sepulchral inscriptions, and in Spain in a few ancient ballads only, for the so-called Spanish Iambic line consists of but eleven syllables.

The Trochaic tetrameter acatalectic has always been a favourite with most versifiers of modern Europe, its two consecutive lines being divided into four, whose alternate final syllables are made to rhyme.

The Greek Lyric, which comprises about thirty various appropriately denominated measures, of diverse forms of construction, would seem to be the parent of all European lyrics ancient and modern, for, amongst them no specimen of versification can be adduced whose prototype is not discoverable amongst passages in the odes of the Hellenic drama. Though this metre may appear to the eye and ear irregular, it is not so in reality, for, were the Strophe and Antistrophe of a Chorale written, separately, in long lines, they would form a tolerable couplet, for they resemble each other in the rhythm and number of feet. Because they have been found, occasionally, to correspond exactly in syllables and quantities, certain commentators have supposed that such regularity was an essential feature in that description of poetry, and, in many instances where no such conformity appears, they have suspected mistranscription in the codices, have altered words to make verses tally, and, by so doing have corrupted the text. *Verrall.* 1887.

Athenæus, Deip. B. 10, c. 80, says that, " in the plays of Callias the Athenian, Strophe and Antistrophe were first introduced ; " that " they had the same melodies and metres ; " and that " Euripides, Sophocles, and other dramatists adopted his system in their Choruses": furthermore, he quotes a Strophe and Antistrophe by Callias, whose syllables and quantities differ materially with one another. As these specimens consist, mainly, of the letters of the alphabet, the probability of a scribe's errors therein seems infinitesimal. The scholiasts on Pindar and Hephæstion, quoted by Gilbert West, speak of arrangement in paragraphs and correspondence in length and measure, but make no mention of parity in syllables and quantities.

The laws of musical progression, when applied to the Lyric metre, verify the assertions of Darley and Brasse that "the *ictus* falls upon the first long syllable of all words therein."

Poetry, in this metre, has the peculiar property of facilitating the expression of various sentiments, which may be illustrated by appropriate musical phrases and cadences of different characters, without interfering with the measured rythm of the verse, whereas, in modern Lyrics, a composer is necessarily restricted to the use of one and the same melody, however unsuitable it may be both for ideas and words.

The poetry in the Greek odes not only conveys to the intelligence ideas of appropriate action and effects of sound, but suggests musical phrases suitable thereto. The same relation which the Fuga has to the Aria, in music, the ancient Lyric has to the modern, in poetry.

The Romans not employing a Chorus at their theatres, when the Hellenic republic sank, the metres of the Greek odes fell by desuetude, and, except in Seneca's tragedies, they have since scarcely ever appeared in any language, though it would seem that Macpherson, to some extent, has employed them in his pseudo Ossianic effusions. The so-called Spanish Anapæstics no wise resemble the Greek Lyrics. There is ample reason why they have become obsolete, for verses written in them were not intended to be recited unaccompanied by pantomime, dance and music. "The poet was acquainted with the art of dancing, so as to keep time with singing; Aristotle states that Telestes, a musical director, in managing the Chorus made all the transactions plain by the dance . . . Every year, at the festival of Bacchus, boys danced in the Chorus to the music of flute-players." *Athenæus, Deip. Ep. B. 1. c. 27. B. 14.*

*b*

*c.* 12. "On the stage, and in the orchestra of Greek theatres, women never appeared." *Francklin's Sophoc :* and *Malone's Shakesp :*

As these ancient lyrics were written to suggest suitable musical phrases, such were especially composed for them ; the poet, therefore, must have introduced certain signs indicating the *pncumata,* breathing points and prolongation of syllables essential to all vocal passages. As there is no notice of such in the texts which have descended to us, no one, however conversant with the Hellenic language, can recite these choral odes so as to impart, or even appreciate their rythm, unless he be an adept in their metres ; but, if anyone, totally unacquainted with them, but familiar with Greek verbal quantities, and possessing a slight knowledge of music, supplies their syllables with equivalent music-indicating notes (*See Mathias's Gr. Gram. v.* 1), and sets the verses in their normal time, $\frac{6}{8}$, the immutable laws of musical progression will at once reveal those rests and minims which will enable him to recite them, as far as rythm is concerned, as correctly as would have a Precentor of an Athenian Chorus. Composers of music employ all the Greek measures, many feet of which, however unrecognizable in ordinary recitation, are distinctly expressible in music. *Callcott's Grammar of Music.*

That, in all cases, the time of these odes should be discovered to be triple is only what we ought to expect, for such is, necessarily, that of the "round dance," and "the Chorus of the Greek theatre received its origin from the *cyclic* (circular) dance of votaries round the altar of Dionusos lighted for his festival ; a belief that the heavenly bodies revolved round the earth having suggested the performance of such sacred ceremony." *Brumoy, Th. Gr.,* the *Orchestra, Davis,* 1603, and *Burton's An. Mel.* The words *Strophe* and *Antistrophe* (turn and back-turn) introduced into the text of the odes, denotes that the movements of the artists therein were circular.

" The *Romaika,* the national dance of the modern Greeks, is circular, and is employed in the religious services of the Passion and the Carnival ; they seldom sing without dancing, and the Strophe and Antistrophe are still in vogue amongst them." *Dodwell's Greece, v.* 2. 18. 32.

" The Encyclic Chorus, the orbicular choir, the circular dance, may be commonly witnessed amongst Greeks of the present period." *Linton's Views in Greece*.

"At the Cathedral of Seville, on every evening during the feast of the Conception, may be witnessed the sacred function of *El baile de los seis*, on which occasion eight boys dressed in blue and white satin, with feathered hats, clinking castanets, dance, in triple time, to music from stringed instruments, before the high altar." *Wells' Antiquities of Spain*. Handel, Latin and Greek laureate at the University of Halle (according to Rockstro), wrote all his dances for votaries in heathen temples, nymphs, and shepherdesses, in triple time.

In the Beggar's Opera, 1728, a medley is suggestive, though in a modern form, of a Greek monode. To Gay's 29 lines in 10 different metres Pepusch adapted 10 popular airs, so skilfully modulated that they glide smoothly on without check.

Lucian, in his tract on the Dance, asserts that "the Greek dialogue on the stage was accompanied throughout by music." "The lines of the Greek dialogue, on the stage, represented a contest between music and poetry." *Belin de Ballu*.

Gibbon, D.F.R.E., cap. 45, quoting Dubois, remarks: "The Gregorian chant has preserved the vocal and instrumental music of the Greek theatre;" but Helmore, in his *Plain Chant*, asserts that the ancient ecclesiastical music was not barred. Francklin, in his Sophocles, supposes that "the music of the Iambic dialogue resembled that of modern opera recitative;" but the Iambic lines are divided into three parts metrically, and absolutely in cæsuras variously placed. Their time, occasionally triple, but never quadruple, is always in sequence irregular, and the recitatives of all operas, old and new, are invariably in fixed time.

It is evident that each Iambic line was sung in a *faux-bourdon* suitable to its measure and matter. In Anglican chants the words of the psalms are drawled out, slurred, and gabbled over in semi and demi-semi quavers, in order to conform to melodies composed without the least reference to them, whereas, for the Greek poetry music being expressly written, each syllable therein was accompanied by a note from the pipe.

Villemain, in his *Cours de la littérature*, "doubts that 'the Iambic dialogue was supported by what would now be called music." He believes that "the piper only sounded in time and in unison with the actor to the syllables of his speech, which he delivered in studied oratorical style;" hence, that the voice of the elocutionist was sustained, his periods impressively marked, and the cadences peculiar to the Hellenic language gracefully adorned.

Thackeray, in a letter to Mrs. Brookfield, states that "in the Roman Senate the voice of an orator was sustained by a pitch pipe."

To the Trochaic tetrameter and the Lyric, which are regular, the former being in long quadruple, and the latter in short triple time, innumerable extant musical phrases are applicable.

Naumann, in his history of Music, tells us that no reliable specimen of Greek music has descended to us. Rockstro, P.M., said on a certain occasion that " the Greek science of music is irretrievably lost;" and that, " were it to be discovered, it would be useless, for its scales, intervals, and inter-relation of notes, were on a system so different to that established in modern times, that musicians would have to unlearn all which they may have previously acquired, and recommence their studies, before they could master it."

Pittman, the *répétiteur*, expressed to the writer his conviction that the said "science, whatever it may have been, never left the sphere of geometricians and theorists," and that "the artists in music must have been acquainted with the properties of the common chord;" and that, " through generations, guilds of them accompanied, instrumentally, by ear;" and that "when the Chorus was no longer employed, their art became extinct."

" Musicam planè pertrectare impossibile." *Macrob. Som. Scip. l. 2. c. 4.* A.D. 380.

" Harmonides, the flute player, said to Timotheus, I owe thee much; thou hast taught me the art of playing correctly . . . . to keep time, to be in tune with the Chorus, to preserve the character of each mode, enthusiasm in the Phrygian, Bacchic fury in the Lydian, and grace in the Ionian." *Lucianus Harmonides, S. 1.* A.D. 150.

In the Choruses it would seem that pipes sounded in unison with voices, accompanied in *arpeggio* by lyres. " Boys played upon the harps, girt up in

xiii

their tunics, singing to the music of the flute, running over all the strings of the harp, at the same time, with the plectrum, in an anapæstic rythm, with a shrill tone. Some played with the plectrum, and some without." *Athenæus Deip. B. 4. c. 17. B. 4. c. 82.* A.D. 160.

Pittman said that "the character and capabilities of the keyless trumpet could not have altered since its invention."

"Sälpĭggŏs āudēn prŏdŏkôn khărădŏkēi." *Eur. Rhes.* "Tūm tŭbă, tērrĭbĭlĭ sŏnĭtū, tărătāntără dĭxĭt." *Ennius.*

"On the ancient stage the length and shortness of every syllable were fixed and determined, either by nature or by use, hence the song had a necessary and agreeable conformity with common discourse, which rendered it more intelligible: our musicians, in the composition of their songs, make short syllables long and long short, as it suits the air or recitative, and, whilst the music pleases the ear, the words frequently offend it." *Francklin's Sophocles.*

"The Greek and Latin tongues assigned, for the pronunciation of each syllable, an exact measure of time, in some longer, in some shorter, and so variously intermixed those two different measures in the same word, as furnished means for that variety of versification to which we are altogether strangers." *Dodsley Miscellanies.*

"Our different cadences, our divisions, variations, repetitions, without which modern music cannot subsist, are entirely improper for the expression of poetry, and were scarce known to the ancients." *Mason's Elfrida.*

Porson, alluding to the works of certain modern popular English poets, remarked that their irregular unscannable verses did not deserve the name of poetry, for no music was suggested by such compositions.

"Without symmetry or harmony, neither the eye nor the ear can be pleased." *Congreve, Preface to Pindar.* See also *Boileau, L'Art Poétique.*

"If genius is to find any expression, it must employ art, for art is the natural expression of our thoughts; the two must go together to form the great painter, poet, or sculptor." *Kavanagh, Longfellow. C. 20.*

Every regular, strictly metrical, lyric cannot fail to offer to a musician a melody of some sort, extant or non-extant; if, in its translation into another language, the number of its syllables, or their quantities, are altered, either no xiv

tune will be suggested, or one different to that intended by the poet, and the lines thus written will bear no resemblance to the original ode. *Tonnelle, Fragments de l'art.* Paris, 1860

" The true element of musical expression is to be found in the accents of the verbal language, which must be correctly rendered in music by the composer." *Grétry, Memoirs,* Paris, 1790.

Upon the subject of the foregoing remarks the following German authors have written extensively, from 1838 to 1885 :—Heimsoeth, Krüger, Bellerman, Westphal, and Van Jan.

In a chapter of the *Cornhill Magazine,* of 1862, Herschell advocates the employment of Greek and Latin metres by English versifiers.

---

In the ensuing translation the Iambic and Trochaic metres are imitated in the same number of feet ; in the Lyric each word is separately represented therein by syllables equivalent in numbers and quantities, and the rules of Greek Prosody are conformed to, in their arrangements.

The linear numeration and disposition, which have been adopted, are those of Paley, without the assistance of whose commentary, and those of Barnes, Böthe and Badham, the following work, such as it is, would not have been attempted by the writer.

---

As various ancient writers have furnished different accounts of the lives of all the characters introduced into this play, an attempt to connect its subject with any so-called history, or even mythological record, would be justly deemed futile and inappropriate.

The year in which, on the Hellenic stage, " Iôn " was first represented, is unknown ; but, from its virulent attacks upon Athenian institutions, we may presume that it was amongst the last of those productions on account of which its author was compelled to quit Attica for ever.

A zealous partisan of liberty, he reproaches the republic for its narrow and selfish policy of withholding from aliens municipal privileges and freedom of speech in public, thereby fostering a monopolist oligarchy, and he taunts it for its pusillanimity in courting the aid of foreign mercenaries in time of war.

He blames it for suffering criminals to find refuge at a sanctuary, and, by implication, for encouraging the priesthood, for the sake of increase to its revenues, in using its influence to promote the success of iniquitous and fraudulent designs.

He professes himself opposed to the employment of serf labour and the traffic in slaves, and alludes to the bad treatment of servants by parvenus.

He evinces his predilection for hereditary monarchy, and recognizes a visible personal distinction between the nobly and the humbly born. He comments severely upon the scant respect paid by the lower to the higher grades of society in Athens.

Why in this, as in other tragedies and comedies, acknowledged Deities were vilified, and popular legends connected with them derided, in the presence of Greek and Roman priests and rulers, with impunity, Père Brumoy suggests a reason. He supposes that " two systems of religion were in vogue amongst them, one mythological and the other theological ; while to ridicule the first was permissible, to disbelieve the second was considered a crime punishable by death."

The Abbé might have pointed his remark by reference to Mysteries and Passion Plays, also to the *Fêtes des Fous* and *de l'Ane*, which, through four hundred years of the Middle Ages in France, were celebrated in cathedrals, publicly, amidst obscenities and profanely parodied sacred rites, in which both the clergy and the laity took part."—*Du Tillot.*

It will scarcely be denied that, in the ensuing play, our poet has exposed himself to just censure by narrating the same story six times. Why has so able and accomplished a writer deliberately violated the ordinary rules of dramatic composition ?

It is noticeable, however, that, whenever the tale is repeated, fresh details are adduced. May it be, as he dwells so on a leading subject, that Euripides, according to Aristophanes an avowed disbeliever in the existence of the

Olympian Gods and the traditions connected with them, desired to demonstrate how, by eliminating the miraculous features from an evidently fabulous legend like that of "Kreousa and Iôn," such may be received as a history of possibly probable events ?

Whatever may be dismissed as supernatural is comprised in the Prologue, wherein the popular fable is appropriately introduced ; all in the drama is natural, and not unlikely to have happened.

In the delusion of Kreousa, who fancies that she has been with child by Apollo, there is surely nothing extraordinary: Joanna Southcote, a single woman of unblemished reputation, who died in 1814, publicly announced her pregnancy with the "*second Shiloh*" ; and, not long ago, as published in the Law Reports, a crazy married lady not only imagined that she was *enceinte* by a certain illustrious personage, but inscribed in her memorandum-book the date of her ideal connection with him. May not the effect of a marvellous dream cause an excitable and ill-regulated mind to lose its balance ?

In the annunciation of an invisible Pallas there is nothing wonderful ; the discovery of the chamber and orifice in the head of the colossal statue of the vocal Memnon, Lightfoot's dissertation on the Jewish "Bath Kol," and Cervantes' account of Moreno's "brazen head," and hence of Friar Bacon's, inform us how voices came from heaven. Pyrotechny was understood, in China, ages before a temple to Apollo was erected. The tricks of performing birds at London music halls eclipse the feats of the trained doves at the Delphic fane.

Kreousa says not that she saw Phoibos in person, aware that, according to popular belief, had he appeared before her she must have perished, but that, when alone, and gathering yellow, gold-eyed crocuses upon the hills near Athens, she perceived advancing towards her a dazzling light, which, from its circular shape, she presumed to be the "golden locks" of that God, with the gold rays on whose statue, at his temple at Makrai, she expresses herself familiar. She declares that she was then dragged into a cavern and outraged.

An unattended damsel in a remote suburb, during the semi-somnolence of a mid-day siesta, indispensable in warm climates, may have been ravished by a swain, whose bright *yellow* hair glittered in sunshine. Similar incidents are described in *Dumas' Mémoires d'un Médecin, Hope's Anastasius, Méry's Frère et Sœur*, and *Ducange's Il y a seize ans*.

Fearing her mother's anger and damage to her reputation, she is silent on the subject of her misfortune, well knowing that no one would credit her account of it. The male child, which she brings forth in secret, is removed from the cave where she deposited it, and she mourns its loss.

The remark of her old slave that her sickness (symptomatic of conception), when noticed, had been a topic of conversation, suggests that the gossip of the servants' hall had reached the ears of the Athenian priests, who, to safeguard the honour of the royal family, transferred the infant to the chiefs of the Delphic temple, who, informed of his illustrious birth, treated him with the highest consideration.

In Webster's tragedy, the secret marriage of the " Duchess of Malfi " is discovered by the same diagnosis, and her babe is abducted from her palace. *Voltaire's L'homme au masque de fer, Quest. Encyc.*, may be here referred to.

Kreousa's marriage with Xouthos proves fruitless. The Athenians ardently desire a descendant of Ericthonios as their future king, well aware that, in default of their queen's issue, a nephew of her husband must, by law, succeed her. The Chorus prays to the Deities to intercede that Kreousa may be blest with a son, and that an alien may never reign over them. We may suppose that the Priests of Pallas fear lest their Goddess's cult should decline, were an Achaian prince to introduce another Deity as their city's patron, and that they resolve to produce the illegitimate heir to the Attic throne. The royal couple repair on pilgrimage to Delphi, to question Phoibos as to their chance of offspring ; and the king-consort halts, on his journey, to make preliminary inquiries at the cave of Trophonios, that seer's officials being, doubtless, prepared to receive him. Hermes intimates that the Delphic prelates have met in conclave, in a recess, to discuss the terms of the forthcoming oracle which, Iôn tells us, Pythia will soon deliver from her tripod. Such pretended divine communication, according to authorities, was conveyed to the Prophetess, while in the crypt, from a cellar beneath it, by the priests, through an orifice from which rose a vapour, most probably of incense.

Xouthos, entering the temple alone, females not being permitted therein, is informed that he shall find a son in the first youth "coming" to meet him as he leaves the nave; and his departure is so timed that the first "youth coming" towards him is the foundling who, as hospitaller, is awaiting him to bid him farewell, and, of course, receive his fees.

The duped prince, supposing that he was the father of the boy by a Mænad, on the occasion of his sole previous visit to Delphi, embraces him as his child, and proposes, in order not to excite the envy of his wife, to introduce him to her as a visitor, and to persuade her to adopt him as her heir.

He names the stripling Iôn, the "coming" man, and commands him to invite his college comrades to supper, and bid them farewell, expressing his intention of performing, in the mountains, sacrifices as a thank-offering. He orders his female servants (the Chorus), under pain of death, to keep his discovery of his son secret from the queen.

His injunctions are disobeyed, and Kreousa, indignant at what she believes her husband's past infidelity and present perfidy, determines to defeat his project of placing his natural offspring upon her throne. She discloses to her attendants what she has so long concealed; she declares that she is, by Apollo, the mother of a boy, of whose whereabouts she is ignorant, but of whose decease she has received no official account. She directs her old slave to poison Iôn.

In what follows, from the alteration in the play's plot as projected by Hermes in the Prologue, we may infer that the priests in Kreousa's train, apprised by their spies of her confession and intentions, deem it necessary to change their tactics. Unaware of her delusion, they had intended, to spare her reputation, to proclaim Iôn's royal birth at some suitable opportunity, when at Athens.

By an incursion of trained doves the queen's murderous design is frustrated; and, by her old slave, under torture, her machinations are revealed. Condemned to death by the Delphic judges, eluding the soldiers sent to arrest her, she hastens, as is expected, for shelter to the sanctuary. Iôn, on arriving there with the town guard, is accosted by the Prophetess, who comes to take leave of him ere his journey to Athens. That she has received her cue from the priests is evident from her exhorting the Hieros, for no valid reason, to save Kreousa's life by exertion of his authority. She exhibits to him, for the first time, the cradle in which she found him on the temple steps. She tells him that in that basket are articles by means of which he may discover his mother. Kreousa, recognizing the pannier in which she had deposited her babe, and correctly specifying its contents ere they are disclosed, convinces Iôn that she who gave him birth stands before him. He at once, exercising his special power in the fane, annuls her sentence, dismisses the guards, and sets her at liberty.

When Iôn is informed by Kreousa that he is the son of his patron Deity, he discredits her statement, although she solemnly swears to it, for he feels confident that it is a blasphemous invention to screen the shame of her seduction by an ignoble swain. Refusing the equivocal position which she offers him, he declares that, determined to learn his father's name, he will, instantly, question upon the subject the God upon his throne in the nave. At this juncture a vivid blaze flashes over the altar, and a voice, professedly that of Pallas, tells the youth that he is the son of Kreousa and Apollo, and that the God has found for him a titular father in order that his welfare may be assured. The same voice orders Kreousa to conduct her boy to Athens, and place him on the throne of his ancestors, but to keep the particulars of his parentage secret, and to suffer Xouthos to continue under the impression that he is the sire of Iôn, for whom a brilliant career is predicted. Firmly believing that he has received a divine annunciation, and that he is submitting to the will of his God, the young prince agrees to accompany his mother to Athens.

Under sacerdotal influence a husband and a wife readily consent to deceive one another; a pious young novice becomes *particeps criminis*, and a gallant soldier is shamefully cajoled. Though, instead of Xouthos palming Iôn upon Kreousa, as was originally intended, Kreousa palms him on Xouthos, the priests of Pallas, aided by those of Apollo, carry their point.

The poet, moreover, enables us to comprehend how an unacknowledged male infant, found upon the steps of a temple, may, as a carnal son of its God, be successfully imposed upon a credulous populace.

The principal character in this play, dedicated in his babyhood to Loxias, is known by no other name but that of " Loxias' boy," and he invokes that

Deity, in public, before his altar, as his " Father." Invested with supreme authority in the fane, of which he is the principal honorary official, he performs especial functions there, and an awful sanctity " hedges " his person. In face and figure he closely resembles the Divinity's statue, like which he is attired and accoutred.

That before, during, and long after Euripides' period the majority of Greeks, as well as Latins, believed in the possibility of a man being the genuine son of an Olympian God there is ample evidence, the incredulity and ridicule of educated and intelligent persons notwithstanding. " Sunt qui Platonem augustiore conceptû prosatum dicant, cum quædam Apollonis figuratio Perictoniâ se miscuisset." *Comm. Casaub.* " Figurationes enim Deorum sunt variæ formæ, quas Dei induere solent, quum mortales convenient." *Hieron. adv. Jovin. l.* 3. " Speusippus, Sororis Platonis filius, et Clearchus et Anaxilides Perictionam, matrem Platonis, phantasmate Apollinis oppressam ferunt et sapientiæ principem non aliter arbitrantur nisi de partû virginis editum." *Apul. de Dogm. Platon. lib.* 1.

" Olympiaden, Philippi uxorem, festivissime rescripsisse legimus Alexandro filio : nam, cum is ad matrem ita scripsisset, Rex Alexander, Jovis Hammonis filius, Olympiadi matri salutem dicit, Olympias ei rescripsit ad hanc sententiam. Amabo, inquit, mi fili, quiescas ; neque deferus me, neque crim:nere adversum Junonem ; malum mihi prosum illa magnum dabit, cum tu me literis tuis pellicem illi esse confiteris." *Aul. Gell. n. a. l.* 13. *c.* 4.

The career of the aforesaid Joanna Southcote passed during the youth of still surviving persons. That, in London, in the nineteenth century, she should have had, from amongst the upper and lower classes of society, and clergymen of the Anglican church, several thousands of followers and abettors who implicitly believed her individual statement that she was an inspired prophetess and future mother of a second Messiah, seems, indeed, astounding. She received pecuniary gifts of such importance that, when invested, they yielded her a handsome revenue ; a magnificent cradle, a superb *layette*, and other costly articles were presented to her for the use of the " coming " babe. The friends of this wretched lunatic, after her decease, suffered her body to remain unburied as long as they were permitted to do so, in the confident expectation that the miraculous infant would manifest itself therefrom. Upon this subject an able writer, in the *Edinburgh Review*, remarks: "The mission of Joanna Southcote is an extremely curious article in the history of human credulity. But, while we laugh at the simplicity of her disciples, we may all of us do well to look homeward—and to consider whether our own belief is not, on various occasions, determined by our feelings more than by evidence—whether we are not sometimes duped by respected names, or bold pretenders—and, sometimes, by our own fancies, fears or wishes." *Evans' Sketch of Sects, Rev. J. Bransby, London, 8vo.* 1841.

---

The ensuing drama has received the warmest approbation from the Fathers of the Christian Church. In modern times the Rev. Joshua Barnes has cited its concluding sentence as "Locum piissimum, certissimæque fidei;" and Père Brumoy, in his *Théâtre de la Grèce*, after lamenting that, for manifest reasons, "Iôn" cannot be produced upon the French stage, has observed that "Though the poet sets us in the midst of the pompous processions and gorgeous ritual of a heathen temple, a deep sentiment of genuine religion pervades his play."

Gibbon, *D. F. R. E. c.* 21, states that "the Hebrew Scriptures were unknown to the Greeks until after the death of Plato;" if his assertion be correct, the resemblance of certain passages in "Iôn" to some in the Old Testament appears remarkable.

---

Two translations of this drama, in metre, respectively by Woodhall and Potter, into English, were published in the years 1781-2, and one in prose by Buckley in 1854.

In 1835 was produced, at Covent Garden Theatre, a tragedy, by Talfourd, entitled "Iôn," the subject of which is an imaginary subsequent career of that mythical personage, to whom its author assigns a parentage and birthplace different to those conceived by Euripides.

---

# IÔN

*OR*

## "THE COMING MAN,"

*A DRAMA BY*

# EURIPIDES,

*IN VERSE,*

ACCOMPANIED THROUGHOUT

BY MUSIC,

*FIRST PERFORMED*

*At the new theatre of Bacchus, (Dionûsos,)*

*AT ATHENS,*

*B.C.* 427 ?

———

" *Aut prodesse solent aut delectare poetæ.*"

## Persons on the Stage.

HERMÈS, *the Deity, in his character of the Gods' messenger.*[1]

PALLAS, *the Deity, in her character of patroness of Athens.*[2]

KREOUSA,[3] *æt.* 33,[4] *queen regnant of Athens.*

XOUTHOS,[5] *a prince of Akhaia,*[6] *husband of Kreousa, king-consort*[7] *of Athens.*

HIEROS,[8] *æt.* 16,[9] *subsequently named* IÔN,[10] *a foundling, Apollôn's daphnêphŏros,*[11] *and, in virtue of such dignity, chief lay-officer of his temple.*[12]

PUTHIA-DELPHIS, *chief priestess and prophetess*[13] *to Apollôn, and principal of the female*[14] *college at Delphi.*

PRESBÛS,[15] *æt. circâ* 85,[16] *a freed slave and confidential male attendant on Kreousa, one who had served her father, during his life, in a similar capacity.*

THERAPÔN,[17] *a freeman and confidential attendant on Xouthos.*[18]

First Prospŏlos,[19] ⎱ *Athenian women, freed slaves and attendants, of the first class,*[20] *on*
Second Prospŏlos, ⎰      *Kreousa.*

---

| | | |
|---|---|---|
| [1] *see l.* 4. | [2] 1554. | [3] *the ruling.* |
| [4] *see* 10. 354. | [5] *the tawny.* | [6] 53. |
| [7] 578. | [8] *the consecrated, so-called* 1252. | [9] 354. |
| [10] 661 *the coming.* | [11] 112. 522 *laurel-bearer.* | [12] 54. |
| [13] 1321. | [14] 1320. *Potter.* | [15] *the old man.* |
| [16] 725. | [17] *servant.* | [18] 1117. |
| [19] *one who goes before, so-called* 510. | | [20] *Athenæus.* |

d

## Mutes.

Therapes,[21] male servants at Apollón's temple.

Two priestesses, who attend to the fire and incense.[22]

Athenian soldiers, as escorts, respectively, to Kreousa[23] and Xouthos.

Delphik soldiers, who represent the town-guard.[24]

Priests, priestesses and townspeople.

## Persons stationed before the logeion.

Khorágos,[25] prompter, poet, conductor of the dialogue, two performers, respectively, on single and double pipes, who accompany[26] the actors in monologue, duologue and dialogue.

## Persons in the Orchestra.

Koruphaios, the conductor of the music of the Khoros.

First and second Khoreutes, Prospóloi to Kreousa, each a vocal leader of a hêmikhoros.

First and second Exarkhos,[27] each a ballet-master of a hêmikhoros.

Forty-six Amphipóloi,[28] Athenian female attendants (of the second class) on Kreousa, who form the Khoros.

---

[21] The term " acolyte " is inadmissible here; it was not applied to temple servants previous to the Christian dispensation.—Communicated by Turner, P.P.

[22] Potter.          [23] 980.          [24] 1266.

[25] provider of the Khoros.          [26] Darley.          [27] Darley.

[28] In A.D. 1787 the Queen of Portugal was attended by sixty ladies-in-waiting.—Beckford. Athenæus.

SCENE.—*Court before the temple of Apollôn Pûthios, at Delphi.*

---

PERIOD.—*A Sunday,[29] towards the end of March,[30] during the Delphinia, the festival of Apollôn, B.C. 1339.[31]*

---

*During the first interlude two hours may be supposed to elapse, during the second, eight. The events, described in the drama, appear to have passed within thirty-six hours.*

---

*The following terms are used in these stage directions : Scena, the stage upon which the practicable and painted scenes rested. Proscenium, a wooden platform, supported by masonry, before the Scena. Logeion, a narrow wooden ledge before the Proscenium. Orchestra, the entire pit of the theatre. Thymelê, a wooden, draped platform, shaped like an altar, before the Logeion, on a level with it, and in the Orchestra. Parödos, one of two semi-circular passages which led from the façade of the theatre, at its extremities, to the Proscenium.*

---

*Some of the dimensions of the theatre of Bakkhos Dionûsos, (where this play was performed,) previous to its demolition during the second and first centuries B.C., judging from those of its extant cotemporaries, may be presumed to have been as follows : length of front, 650 ft. ; length of stage, 300 ft. ; depth, including logeion, 75 ft. ; diameter of orchestra, 150 ft. ; width of parödos, 15 ft. ; height, 29 ft.*

---

[29] 420. *Hesiod—Plutarch.*      [30] *Clinton.*      [31] *Bell.*

*The Koruphaios remains standing on the thymelê during the whole of the action of the drama, and conducts the music of the Khoros; also takes a part in the dialogue, not as a performer, but as one who represents the audience. The Khoros, likewise, maintains its position in the orchestra until the conclusion of the play; some of its members are flutists, others lyrists and vocalists; all are dancers. With ballet and pantomime they illustrate both words and incidents throughout; and their odes are accompanied by their own instruments. The actors on the stage recite, only in unison with the notes of the pipers who are stationed immediately below them."*[33]

[33] *The foregoing paragraph is compiled from Francklin's preface to his Sophocles.*

## SCENE.

*The inner court before the temple of Apollôn Puthios, at Delphi, whose 'practicable'*

## ERRATA.

Page xx, Line 20, *for* deferus *read* deferas
  „  8,  „  19, *for* panier *read* pannier
  „  9,  „  33, *for* Delphir *read* Delphoi
  „  14,  „  167, *for* thine *read* thy
  „  43,  „  681, *for* But, *read* Say,
  „  69,  „  1250, *for* Prospolloi, *read* Prospoloi,
  „  77,  „  1387, *for* panier's *read* pannier's
  „  95, Note 54, *for* Nicœa *read* Nicæa
  „  99,  „  124, *for* Pœan *read* Pæan
  „  101,  „  175, *for* Œstuat *read* Æstuat

*the surrounding precipices, the stage to be in twilight.*

## PROLOGUE.

*After a peal of thunder, Hermes descends from the scenic clouds, upon a pendulum rope steadied by an iron weight at a distance of two feet from the floor. In circular motion, this rope being coiled round his left leg, with his right hand waving his*

1

*The Koruphaios remains standing on the thymelê during the whole of the action of the drama, and conducts the music of the Khoros; also takes a part in the dialogue, not as a performer, but as one who represents the audience. The Khoros, likewise, maintains its position in the orchestra until the conclusion of the play; some of its members are flutists, others lyrists and vocalists; all are dancers. With ballet and pantomime they illustrate both words and incidents throughout;*

## Scene.

*The inner court before the temple of Apollón Puthios, at Delphi, whose 'practicable' front, in the Doric style, is represented as in white marble, upon a terrace approached by steps. In the double colonnade, which forms the peristyle, are altars backed by statues of the following deities, Zeus, Poseidón, Bakkhos, Pan, Artemis, Pallas, Leto, and the Mousai; also vases containing laurel and myrtle shrubs. The metopes, between the triglyphs on the outer frieze, are sculptured in alt-relief; the continuous subjects on the inner frieze are in bas-relief, and the statues in the tympanum of the pediment are entire. All these sculptures are tinted, and are supplied with metallic appurtenances. The principal entrance is flanked by two smaller doorways. Portions of walls, furnished with gates, form the side scenes. The doors and gates are of gilt bronze. In the centre of the stage, elevated by steps, is a large altar from which ascend a flame, and smoke from standard censers thereon. The fire and incense are kept alight, during the drama, by two priestesses, who occasionally enter from the temple for that purpose. Behind this altar, and in front of the Stoa, on a terraced pedestal is a colossal statue of Phoibos, draped. (This image of the Delphic God is stated by Dodwell and Canova to have been the prototype of that known as the Apollo-Belvedere, to have been of bronze gilt, its head crowned with laurel and surrounded by gold rays, and bearing bow and quiver.) On a painted scene, on the left of the spectator, are delineated distant temples and palaces, and on the right, part of the mountain range of Parnassos. The time is supposed to be that of early morning, but the sun not having yet risen above the surrounding precipices, the stage to be in twilight.*


## Prologue.

*After a peal of thunder, Hermes descends from the scenic clouds, upon a pendulum rope steadied by an iron weight at a distance of two feet from the floor. In circular motion, this rope being coiled round his left leg, with his right hand waving his*

I

*caduceus, and with his left, by concealed springs, fluttering the wings on his cap and ankles, he reaches the stage and advances to the logeion.*

HERMES, *to audience.*                                                *Iambic.*

Atlâs (whose brazen shoulders toil to turn the old
domain of Gods, the Heav'ns,) by his celestial wife
a daughter had, hight Maia, who to mighty Zeus
bore *me*, Hermês, as henchman Daimŏnes to serve.—
To Delphik land I've come where Phoibos, thron'd at Earth's
core's entry, chanting hymns for mortals' benefit,
what present is, what was, and what's to be declares.—
In Hellas stands a town which, (not ignor'd by Fame,)
with gold-spear-wielding Pallas its cognomen hath;
there, whilom, Phoibos ravish'd young Kreousa, child
of King Erektheus, 'mongst the northern rocks by all
the magistrates of Atthis' country styl'd " Măkrai,
" Athênai-Pallădon's defence impregnable."—
Kreousa's womb a burthen felt and, when arriv'd
her time, at home, unwatch'd she gave the God a boy;
her father wist not of't, for so it pleas'd the Lord.
In that same cave where by the God she'd been deflow'r'd
her suckling she depos'd, as if for Death design'd,
inside a wicker panier semicircular,
ancestral rites conforming to; (Erìkthŏnios,
engender'd by the soil, when issuing thence, receiv'd,
from Zeus' wise virgin, guards in serpents twain; she sent
Agraulis' maidens three enjoin'd to shield him well
from harm: a custom, hence, that monarch's noble race
observes of rearing all its progeny bedeck'd
with gold snake-ornaments;) the trinkets which she wore
this girl clasp'd round the neck of bantling left to die.—
My brother Phoibos straight invok'd and charg'd me thus—
" To bright Athênai fly, my cognate, (well thou mind'st

" the Goddess' burgh, where Gaia human broods produc'd,)      30
" there, 'mongst the hollow'd crags, a new-born baby find:
" in 'ts swaddle gear, in 'ts bassinet, with all therein,
" to Delphir waft it, reach my seat oracular,
" and safely set it down before the temple-doors !
" For what remains (assur'd be thou that mine it is,)      35
" my care shall be."—This grace at once to Loxias
accorded was; I cleft the air, I rais'd aloft
the woven ark, and deftly plac'd it 'fore the nave's
front steps, neglecting not the basket's lid to leave
wide-open, so that well the infant might be 'spied.—      40
When Hêlios' coursing disc appear'd, the Prophetess
discern'd it there as tow'rds the presage-crypts she stroll'd:
she threw a glance amaz'd upon the hapless waif,
and marvell'd much that dar'd some Delphik damsel had
clandestine birth to fling before the Lord's abode:      45
at first, beyond the precincts she to cast it wish'd,
but Pity over Cruelty prevail'd: (the God
from hearth of his the bairn's expulsion help'd to thwart:)
she lifted up and nurs'd him; who his mother is
she ne'er hath heard, ne'er guess'd that Phoibos him begot.—      50
Anent his parentage no inkling hath the youth;
round altars spread with food, when grown a sprightly chit,
he frisk'd in wheedling guise; on manhood ere he verg'd,
by Delphik chiefs was he their God's sole sacristan,
prime warden, bursar too appointed; 'neath the roof      55
of that God's house he's led, till now, a holy life.—
Kreousa, she who brought this stripling forth to light,
Duke Xouthos' bride became soon after that event:
he, when Athênai's troops with Khalkŏdontïdes,
Euboia's isle who dwell in, wag'd a bitter war,      60
to Atthis' soldiers lent his lance, subdued the foe,
and priceless guerdon won in fair Kreousa's hand:

no indigene, Akhaion native he, ysprung
from Aiŏlos, of Zeus a scion ; long espous'd,
no heir have he and his Kreousa ; hence they seek,                    65
on pilgrimage, Apollôn's fane to counsel ask,
for offspring longing,—Marks th' occasion Loxïas ;
(he hides not this from *me*, although he thinks he does ;)
by special spell he'll grant to Xouthos, when he quits
the shrine, this springal, let that prince believe that he's          70
his sire, and guide him straight to his maternal halls,
agniz'd to be by queen Kreousa.—Secret will
be Phoibos' union kept, and much shall gain the lad ;
for him the God will cause in Asia realms to found,
him (dubb'd the "coming man,") in Hellas make renown'd.—              75
The Daphnê-garlanded recess I'll steal within,
learn, touching this said foundling, what new scheme's afoot.—
I see from out the cella Loxias' son approach
on all this dome's refulgent portals wreaths to hang
of laurel branches : soon by th' name shall he be known              80
which I'm the first of Gods to bruit abroad—IÔN.

*Exit* HERMES *by side scene gate.   A peal of thunder is heard.*

*End of prologue.*

### EPISODE.

*Enter, by left parodos, to the proscenium, and descend to the orchestra:* KORUPHAIOS, *followed by the Khoros, represented by the amphipoloi of Kreousa: it files off in two columns, (Hemikhoroi,) each of which is preceded by its First Khoreutes and Exarkhos. These two companies station themselves on each side of the thymele, which Koruphaios mounts.*

*The sun is now to be supposed to rise above the mountains' tops. Enter, from the principal gate of the temple,* HIEROS. *Crowned with a laurel wreath, and bearing bow and quiver, he is masked and attired to resemble the statue of Apollôn on the stage. He advances to the proscenium and indicates to the audience, successively, the painted scene and façade of the nave.*

### ODE I. *Monôdê* I.

HIEROS, *to audience.*                                                    *Lyric.*

      See, from on high, 'mid a lustre resplendent,
      Hêlios urge car four-hors'd to the earth !
      See what a fire sends stars fro' the sky, in a
          flight, Nûx to rejoin !                                 85
      Parnêsos, on heads which we ne'er can a'proach,
      With a glow from his wheels' bright glare is ablaze,
      Ere men get a glimpse of a day's dawn.—
      Smyrnese resin up to the God's părăpèts
          puffs smoke in a cloud,                                 90
      and, thron'd on a weird trĭpŏd, is the devote,
      Delphis who'll, 'mongst crowds Hellênik, aloud,
          chant a refrain voic'd by Apollôn.

*(Enter, from side-scene gates,* THERAPES *adult and juvenile, with five slaves bearing on their heads baskets of laurel boughs; having worshipped the statue of Phoibos, they decorate the nave's doors, under the inspection of* HIEROS *who, when their task is completed, mounts the altar steps and summons them.)*

      Ho there, Delphoi, Phoibos' thĕrăpĕs !

(THERAPES *form into ranks before the altar.*)

Hear! Kastălĭě's silvery cool font        95
Speedily march tow'rds! By the rills in her well
When ye all be refresh'd, back to the nave wend!
Pious words, well tim'd, take care to pronounce,
bland speech be to all those who a'rive and
     seek our God's spell,       100
but couch an a'dress in a choice phrase!

(*Exeunt, by left parodos,* THERAPES *in marching order.*)
HIEROS (*to audience*)

And mine be the task (which, from child's age,
I've daily achiev'd), discreetly to clear
the a'proach to the dome with a blest bay's wreaths,
with a pure lymph, from a tank, floors to asperge   105
i' the house o' the Lord, and birds in a flock,
    (lest such soil rich
gifts of a vot'ry,) by shafts, sped from a bow,
to repel warily!—Since not a parent,
nor a kin to obey I've known, Phoibos'      110
fane (mine own home,) my devòirs claims.—

(*Here he approaches the vases in the peristyle, and with shears cuts laurel and myrtle branches therefrom.*)

    Be pluck'd ye marve'lous, young,     *Strophè.*
use-fraught shoots from a lovely Daphnê,
gemm'd shrines all well do ye cleanse
round nave to my Lord rais'd!       115
Your green groves fade not away,
in which benign drops, still'd from a source
ne'er exhausted, aye keep moist
    leaves of a hallow'd
Mûrsĭnê in a dew serene!—       120
With these swept be thy paths, my God!—

When Hêĕlïos, in air, on a flight's visible, my task,
    begun, lasts til' he sinketh.

*(Having formed the branches into wreaths, with them he sweeps the altar and pavement,
then kneels before the statue of Apollôn and adores it in monotone.)*

        O Paiân, o Paiân,
        euaiôn, euaiôn                   125
        bless thee, ô Lêtô's son!
        The toil's a joy, for a serf,       *Antistrophè.*
Phoibos, I'm to thy dome! My God's spell,
psalms, lauds I sing to thy seat!

    *(Here he rises and addresses the audience.)*

Brave work! What a boon 'tis              130
to humble slave be to the Gods,
(not men,) those who taste not o' death!
Ne'er, ne'er let mĕ desert such grand,
such a renown'd post!—
Phoibos *me* as a sire protects;           135
one that rears me my praise deserves!

    *(Here he again kneels before the altar.)*
So I'm dutiful when *I*, in a hymn, call on, as a Sire,
    Phoibos, thron'd in a temple!—
        O Paiân, ô Paiân,
        euaiôn, euaiôn             140
        bless thee, ô Lêtô's son!

    *(Here he rises and addresses the audience.)*    *Epôdê.*
    But now I'll pause from shearing
        Daphnê's twigs for
    brooms to pour pure, earth-produc'd lymph from
      fresh-fill'd gold urns,
    (lymph which hath well'd far-fam'd      145
      Kastălïê's spring), and

shed it in our aisles. (*Aside, crossing his arms
on his breast, and bending his knee before the altar*,) Chaste's this
body, for in heart I'm pure.

(*Here he kneels, and prays to the statue, in monotone*.)

   Ne'er, ne'er let mĕ cease, Phoibos,    150
 to serve this fane, this dear shrine, save
 cease I, call'd to the grac'd part act——

(*Here, as an eagle flies towards the temple, he starts up*.)

    Eàh! Eàh!
 Birds swoop down who've eyries just left
 'mongst those [steep] Parnêsos' rock-clefts!  155

   (*He strings and adjusts his bow*.)

 Halt, I say! Spare these ramparts!
 These gold deck'd walls keep far from!
 *Thee* shall darts pierce through, Zeus' herald,
 *thee* whose seres o'er fowls' whole race gain
    sov'reign conquest!—    160

(*He shoots, the eagle falls, and a swan appears, chirruping*.)

To the God's thŭmĕlês straineth amain some
   cygnet! Hark! Wilt those
 legs, purple in hue, not at once sheer off?
 Phoibos' lyre, that chirp though tun'd with,
 *thee* shall not save from bolt-points keen!  165
    So revers'd be thy wings,
 hie back to thine own lake Dêliadŏn!
 An' mindest not these wise words,
 life's blood will flow 'mid sweet songs!

(*Having killed the swan, he espies a swallow*.)
    Eàh! Eàh!      170
 Who is here now? What bird new to the sky?

*Would* she, for young chicks' neat, warm nests,
'neath these eaves mass straw-fragments ?
Check thee strong, loud-twang'd bow-string !

(*He shoots, and misses his aim.*)

Art warn'd not ?   Callow brood would'st rear,
seek Alpheus' swift deep whirlpools,                    175
else [some] thicket Isthmïon !—

(*Hawks, storks and herons appearing, he scares them away by discharging repeated volleys of arrows.*)

Here let our images all rest stain-free,
Phoibos' shrines likewise !—

(*He watches the retreating flocks.*)

(Shame though feel I birds [thus] slaught'ring;
birds bring mortals great Gods' solemn              180
mandates.)—All these functions charg'd with,
Phoibos serve must I—

(*Here enter, by left parodos,* FIRST *and* SECOND PROSPOLOS.   HIEROS, *perceiving them approaching the temple, advances, as hospitaller, to receive them.*)

and ne'er fail
those off'ring gifts to a'tend on.—

FIRST PROSPOLOS, *indicating the temple and painted scene, to* SECOND PROSPOLOS.
Ode 2. *Monostrophica—Lyric.*                    *Strophè* 1.

Gaze round! Boast can alone Athê-
nai nave rais'd (with a nobly carv'd              185
porch) to Gods, or a shrine wi' sta-
tue su'plied for a street-cult ?

(*Indicating a temple of Artemis, painted on the scene.*)

Phoibos here has a temple; here,
too, fronts twain of a fane to Lêtô's chaste daughter our eyes daze !

(HIEROS, *having accosted the women, proceeds to exhibit to them the temple's exterior.*
*He points with his bow to the metopes on the outer frieze, and describes them, in a*
*long-drawn conventional chant.*)

HIEROS *to* PROSPOLOI,

> Regard this design, first;                                                          190
> Lernaion Hŭdrê destroy'd, with
> gold-bedight, curv'd sword, by the Zeus' son!

FIRST PROSPOLOS, *to* SECOND (*who is watching* HIEROS, *with the intention of*
*making game of him*),

> My dear, what he shows glance at!

SECOND PROSPOLOS,

> We see't.                                                                            *Strophè* 2.

HIEROS, *continuing,*

> Near him is other he-
> ro, who grasps in his hand a fire-                                                   195
> brand—

SECOND PROSPOLOS, *abruptly, to* HIEROS,

> How is he yclep'd?

FIRST PROPOLOS, *to* SECOND, *reproachfully,*

> The tale's
> told, thou know'st, by my own loom.

HIEROS,

> Shield-arm'd mail'd Iolâos here
> shares, with laudable zeal, the toil
> severe borne by the Zeus' son.—                                                      200

> (*Indicating a second metope.*)
> And this note! A brave man
> bestrideth a wingéd war-steed,
> and slay'th a ghastly, trïfòrm'd beast,
> a monster who fire breathes!

SECOND PROSPOLOS (*again rebuked and mimicking* HIEROS' *chant*),

> Sure, all round mĕ revolve my eye-balls!                          *Strophè* 3. 205

HIEROS (*pointing to the statues in the pediment*),

> Look where, in a rout, (hewn from a
> rock,) battle Gigantes!

(*Beckoning to the women to approach him.*)

Friends, from here can we view them all!

> (*To* FIRST PROSPOLOS.)
> See'st who glares on Enceladòs?
> See'st who flaunts her buckler, aloft?            210

*Both* PROSPOLOI,

> Ay, our Pallăs ador'd we 'spy!

HIEROS,

> What else?

FIRST PROSPOLOS *to* SECOND,

> A double
> bolt, fiery, thundery, Zeus, with a
> propulsive hand, has hurl'd forth!

SECOND PROSPOLOS,                                     *Strophè* 4.

> We see't

HIEROS,

> Huge, grim, fierce Mĭmâs to
> ashes he means to burn!—            215
> Note Brŏmios use an
> i'nocuous, wreath'd with ivy, light mace
> to strike stone-dead a son o' Gaiê!

SECOND PROSPOLOS, *abruptly, affecting rustic simplicity,*

> My guide, thou who the temple-door guard'st,
> can *I* to the aisles within pass,            220
> on bar'd feet?   Prithee—

HIEROS, *startled,*

> Bars ye the Law, my guests!

SECOND PROSPOLOS,

> May'n't I ask thee, my host, at least, some questions?

HIEROS,

Upon what wou'd ye ask?

SECOND PROSPOLOS (*glibly*), *Strophè* 5.

I' this dome, to the midst of Earth
straight entrance can a gate a'ford?
Fenc'd by the wreaths is it? Watch'd by the Gorgŏnĕs?

HIEROS,

Yes, dame.  (*Aside*) So it is oft said. 225

(*Aloud, citing an inscription on the temple-wall.*)

" If ye but offer a [cake] as a gift at a pyre,
" when ye would Phoibos' oracle ask aught,
" to the shrine can ye go.—If ye come sans well-
" grown sheep, not a hope raise to the nave visit!"—

FIRST PROSPOLOS (*gravely*),

Aware am I, Sir. 230
Abide we by the rules of a Deity!
The outer walls the eyes charm!

HIEROS *to* SECOND PROSPOLOS, *Epôdê.*

All can ye see, which ye ought, at a sanctu'ry!

SECOND PROSPOLOS, *pretending to whimper*,

My patrons sent me here to scan the
" guala," the God's recess!

HIEROS, *losing patience*,

Whence come ye to me?
whose girls can ye be?

(*Here a flourish of trumpets from without.*)

SECOND PROSPOLOS, *offended, haughtily*,

Pallădŏn we style that 235
palace on a rock which own my fam'd Tŭrannoi.
Demand aught else from one who here comes!

*Enter by left parodos,* KREOUSA, *wearing a " weeping mask," and preceded by trumpeters and bearers of the Athenian standard the " Grasshopper," and followed by a guard of honour. All pay reverence to the altar, except* KREOUSA, *who appears overcome by grief at the sight of it. The attendants then stand in rows before the scene, and* HIEROS, *advancing, ceremoniously receives the queen.*

HIEROS *to* KREOUSA,                                                   *Iambic.*

     Whoe'er thou art, thy grand deportment plainly shows
     that thou, my lady, well may'st claim a lineage high !
     From manner, shape and gait, by many signs, we know
     if noble be, or humble, birth of those we meet.—            240

     *(Approaching* KREOUSA, *he notices her weeping mask and agitation.)*

              Eàh !
     Amaz'd am I to see thy gloomy countenance,
     thine eyes half clos'd, and comely cheeks with tears suffus'd,
     as gazest thou on Loxias' seat oracular!

     *(He indicates an inscription on the pediment's architrave.)*

     Why com'st thou here with carking care surcharg'd, my dame,
     for " all, who view the God's abode, with holy zeal             245
     " rejoice," but thou, absorb'd in woe, survey'st the shrine ?
KREOUSA,
     I freely grant thee, sir, of reason there's enough
     that thou should'st wonder what constrains me thus to weep.—
     Beholding Lord Apollôn's gorgeous temple-dome
     of certain past events the mem'ry sad recalls,                 250
     and homewards flies my mind, though here my body stands.—
  *(Aside)* Oh, wretched womankind ! Oh, outrage scandalous
     by Gods ! But where's redress ? For justice where to seek,
     if we from those who rule us suffer cruel wrong ?
HIEROS,
     What latent matter, madam, grieveth so thy heart ?            255

KREOUSA *(aside)*,

    I've launch'd but aimless shafts! *(Aloud)* Of that no question ask,
    no further notice take!—I speak of it to none.

HIEROS, *producing, from his sinus, tablets and style,*.

    But who art *thou?* From what far land arriv'st, my dame?
    What name may we address thee by? How styl'st thy sire?

KREOUSA,

    Erektheus' daughter, queen Kreousa call'd am I:          260
    Athênê's town, my native place, my home remains.

HIEROS, *with courteous gesture,*

    Such splendid city dwelling in, from princely sires
    descended, thee, ô gracious stranger, I revere!

KREOUSA,

    In those, not other, chances blest am I, my host.

HIEROS,

    Oh, say, by all the Gods, is true what men relate—        265

KREOUSA,

    What is't, young sir, thou show'st such eagerness to know?

HIEROS, *continuing,*

    that thy renown'd forefather sprung direct from Earth?

KREOUSA,

    Erìkthŏniôs came thence. *(Aside)* Nought's worth my race to me.

HIEROS,

    And did Athênê lift him up from off the ground?

KREOUSA,

    Ay, 'tween her virginal arms. A mother ne'er she was.     270

HIEROS,

    As pictures represent, entrusted she the child—

KREOUSA,

    To Cèkrôps' girls to guarded be, unseen, by them.

HIEROS,

    'Tis said his daughters dar'd the Goddess' ark to ope.

KREOUSA,
> For which, enforc'd to die, with blood they ting'd the rocks?

HIEROS,
> Just so.—
> Pray, tell me, dame, is true or false a tale we hear?      275

KREOUSA,
> What would'st enquire about?    At leisure quite am I.

HIEROS,
> Thy sisters did thy sire Erektheus sacrifice?

KREOUSA,
> Those maidens he, as victims, slew to save the land.

HIEROS,
> And how was't *thou*, amongst them all, alone preserv'd?

KREOUSA,
> In arms maternal I, a new-born baby, lay.      280

HIEROS,
> Thy father, caught by gaping soil, engulph'd was he?

KREOUSA,
> By awful Pontos' three prong'd sceptre's stroke he died.

HIEROS,
> Is call'd Măkrai the site of that catastrophè?

KREOUSA, *angrily,*
> To what remembrance hateful brings why should'st allude?

HIEROS, *astonished,*
> By Pûthion halo-rays and Pûthios grac'd it is!      285

KREOUSA,
> 'Tis " grac'd "! How " grac'd " is it? Would *I*'d ne'er seen the cliffs!

HIEROS, *terrified,*
> What say'st?    Because my God esteems it, loath'st a rock?

KREOUSA,
> No, no!    Within its caves I wot of guilty deeds.—

HIEROS, *after a pause, during which he writes on his tablets,*
> Amongst Athênai's people, princess, who's thy spouse?

KREOUSA,

No Atthis' man ; from other clime evok'd was he.  290

HIEROS, *aside*,

Of some good stock he needs to be.   (*Aloud*) What name is his ?

KREOUSA,

Xouthos.   He's son of Aiŏlos whom Zeus begot.

HIEROS,

As alien, how could *he* wed *thee*, an indigene ?

KREOUSA,

Euboia our Athênai's neighbour boasts to be.

HIEROS,

" A wat'ry frontier bounded by," as well they say.  295

KREOUSA,

With lance he join'd the Cĕcrŏpĭdês, and spoil'd the isle.

HIEROS,

Came he as their ally, and found in thee a bride ?

KREOUSA,

His battle's prize, his conq'ring spear's reward was I.

HIEROS,

Escorteth thee thy lord, or seek'st this shrine alone ?

KREOUSA,

From fam'd Trophônios' cave my husband I await.  300

HIEROS,

The marvels scans he there, or question asks the seer ?

KREOUSA,

From him and Puthios same reply he hopes to hear.

HIEROS,

For fruitful land, or offspring, come ye here to pray ?

KREOUSA,

Though married long we've been, no issue have we yet.

HIEROS,

What ?   Childless art thou ?   Ha'st thou ne'er a baby borne ?  305

KREOUSA, *glancing at Phoibos' statue,*
>That *I've* no infant nurtur'd Phoibos knoweth well.

HIEROS,
>Ah, luckless wife, though bright's thy state, how dark's thy lot!

KREOUSA, *gazing alternately upon* HIEROS *and the statue,*
>But who art *thou ?* (*Aside*) I ween she's blest who caus'd thy birth.

HIEROS,
>I'm styl'd this Deity's " Slave," your grace, for such am I.

KREOUSA,
>Was't bought from traders here, or by this city giv'n ?          310

HIEROS,
>All call me " Loxias' boy"; no more's beknown to me.

KREOUSA,
>Alas, poor youth, 'tis now my turn to pity thee——

HIEROS,
>As one who ne'er a mother, ne'er a sire beheld ?

KREOUSA,
>Within this temple dwell'st, or 'neath some friendly roof?

HIEROS,
>My God's whole house is mine, whene'er I list to sleep.          315

KREOUSA,
>As child, or lad, wast brought to these prophetic halls ?

HIEROS,
>As new-born suckling, those declare who ought to know.

KREOUSA,
>Whose milk, 'mongst Delphik wives, thine instant need supplied ?

HIEROS,
>No female bosom met my lips, but nurs'd was I——

KREOUSA,
>By whom, ô hapless waif? (*Aside*) Fresh anguish racks my breast!   320

HIEROS, *continuing,*
>by her whom call'd I " mother," Phoibos' prophetess.

3

KREOUSA,

 And how, through childhood passing, didst thou gain thy meals?

HIEROS,

 My food at shrines, from sundry pilgrims doles had I.

KREOUSA,

 A wretch is she who brought thee forth, whoe'er she be!

HIEROS,

 Belike, to some fine lady's shame conceiv'd was I.     325

KREOUSA, *starting, then assuming indifference,*

 What means are thine to spend, for sumptuous seems thy dress?

HIEROS, *indicating his carcanet, baldrick, &c.,*

 To th' God, whose serf am I, this garb, these gems, belong.

KREOUSA,

 And who thy parents are didst never strive to learn?

HIEROS,

 Woe's me, of them, dear madam, none perceive a trace.

KREOUSA, *sighing,*

 Phew!

 A certain woman's plight thy mother's matcheth well.    330

HIEROS,

 Her sympathy would cheer me much!  To whom refer'st?

KREOUSA,

 To her on whose account preceded is my spouse.

HIEROS,

 That I may aid thee, dame, say, what desir'st to do?

KREOUSA,

 To Phoibos questions ask on secrets known to none.

HIEROS,

 An' tell'st me more, thy proxĕnos I'll gladly be!     335

KREOUSA,

 Then hear my tale, but—Aidôs warneth me to pause!

HIEROS,

 Nay, heed not her!  That Goddess here no mission hath.

KREOUSA,
>That she with Phoibos lay a friend of mine avers——

HIEROS, *shocked*,
>A mortal maid with Phoibos?  Say not, lady, that!

KREOUSA, *continuing*,
>and, sans her father's knowledge, gave the God a boy.                340

HIEROS, *vehemently*,
>It cannot be!  By man seduc'd she feels asham'd.

KREOUSA,
>" Not so," said she, and—suffer'd much that blighted wench——

HIEROS,
>From what?  (*Aside*) Who'll e'er believe that next a God she lay?

KREOUSA,
>She carried forth from home the child she brought to light.

HIEROS,
>And where's the nursling thus discarded?  Lives he still?                345

KREOUSA,
>That no one knows; I've come, to ask that question, here.

HIEROS,
>Is cause to deem him dead, if so, by what mishap?

KREOUSA,
>She fancies savage beasts her helpless birth devour'd.

HIEROS,
>What evidence induc'd her such event to fear?

KREOUSA,
>She went where laid he'd been, but found him there no more.                350

HIEROS,
>And saw she clotted blood whose gouts had stain'd the floor?

KREOUSA,
>" No drop," quoth she, though " oft and oft she search'd it o'er."

HIEROS,
>And since she lost her son, how much of times elaps'd?

KREOUSA,

Survive did he, like thine would bloom his downy cheeks.

HIEROS,

And have not since been other children granted her ?   355

KREOUSA,

The God's unjust to that sad dame, for none she hath.

HIEROS,

But what would'st say, had Phoibos rear'd the bairn by stealth ?

KREOUSA,

Unfair 't had been to take of common joy the whole.

HIEROS,

Ah, me !   That outcast's case with mine seems parallel !

KREOUSA,

I trow thy woeful mother longs for thee, my guide.   360

HIEROS, *sobbing*,

Perhaps.—Of griefs I'd fain forget remind me not !

KREOUSA,

I'll speak of them no more.—Proceed with thy remarks !

HIEROS,

Do'st note the chief impediment to thy design?

KREOUSA,

What ills may not that stricken female yet betide ?

HIEROS,

Why should the God disclose what most he'd wish to hide ?   365

KREOUSA,

On Hellas' common tripod he sits ; he can't refuse.

HIEROS,

Ne'er question him on what would cause him shame to feel !

KREOUSA,

I must : her dire misfortune sorely wastes my friend.

HIEROS, *mounting the altar steps*,

No priest will make for thee a query like to this !—

Reproach'd with vilest crimes beneath his temple-roof,　　　　370
with reason Phoibos would his words' interpreter
severely treat.—O queen, this project vain renounce!—
Let none presume to pester Gods averse to hear!—
Of human follies all, believe me, 'tis the worst
'mongst carcases of beasts on altars sacrific'd,　　　　375
or passing flocks of birds, for omens fair to seek,
and importùne the Gods, if loth they be to speak.—
Know this!　When unpropitious Gods we supplicate
for worldly good, if gain'd it often proves a bane,
my guest, while what they grant unsought brings benisons!　　　380

> *Having made reverence to the altar, he descends its steps.*

KORUPHAIOS, *to audience,*
We mortals num'rous are, and our untow'rd mishaps
in life as num'rous are; in various forms they come,
but one unmix'd good-hap by rarest chance appears.

> *Here* KREOUSA *ascends the altar steps, and passionately addresses the
> statue of* PHOIBOS, *without genuflexion or reverence.* HIEROS *watches
> her with alarm and astonishment.*

KREOUSA, *to the statue,*
Unjust art thou to her who speaks before thee here,
ô Phoibos, ay, unjust to her who weeps at home!　　　　385
No care thou show'd'st the boy to whom thy care was ow'd,
nor tell'st his mother e'en, omniscient though thou art,
if dead he be, that he in seemly tomb be laid,
or if alive he be, that mother's eyes to cheer!

> *(After a pause, she turns her back upon the altar, with scorn, and descends.)*

Then, since this God withholds what most I wish to know,　　　390
forthwith prepare must I elsewhere to make research.

(*A flourish of trumpets is heard from without, and enter, by left parodos,*
XOUTHOS, *attended by trumpeters and guard of honour.*)

KREOUSA, *to* HIEROS,

 Now, gentle youth, my noble consort I descry!
 from sage Trophônios' fane prince Xouthos marcheth here!—
 I've secrets told; speak nought of them before my spouse,
 lest, in a tale of shame and sorrow not my own,      395
 to sense at variance quite with what I meant, my words
 distorted be, and serious mischief me befall!
 'Mongst men we feeble women lead uneasy lives,
 for females good and bad by Fame commingled are;
 mistrusted hence, we're all in nature born to woe.     400

XOUTHOS, *advancing,*

 My salutations, first, to yonder God be paid
 in humble rev'rence!  (*He kneels before* PHOIBOS' *statue, then
  rises and embraces* KREOUSA.)   Next, my dear wife, hail to thee!
 (*observing her agitation and weeping mask*),
 Say, hath my long delay'd arrival caus'd alarm?

KREOUSA, *to* XOUTHOS, *tenderly,*

 No, no, thou com'st while other cares engage my thoughts—
 of wise Trophônios' answer tell me, ô my love!     405
 Of soon producing offspring, say, what chance have we?

XOUTHOS,

 T' anticipate this God's response oracular
 unmeet he deem'd, but said that neither thou, nor I,
 should quit this shrine and homeward wend without a son.

KREOUSA, *kneeling before the statue of Lêtô, in the peristyle.*

 O Phoibos' sainted mother, favour'd if we come     410
 with lucky omens, may our union soon (*aside*) (the first,
 thy son's and mine I mean,) (*aloud*) more happiness afford!

XOUTHOS, *devoutly, to* KREOUSA,

 So be't!  (*perceiving* HIEROS *approach to receive him, officially.*)
   Who's here?  Is't he who questions asks the God?

HIEROS, *to* XOUTHOS.

 Outside the God's Recess I serve; therein preside
 the Delphik chiefs, sire; next the Trĭpŏd, on thrones they sit,  415
 by lot elected they their sacred office hold.

XOUTHOS, *to* HIEROS,

 'Tis well; I'm now inform'd on all I wish'd to know.—
 I'll pass within, because I'm told a sacrifice
 especial, 'fore the nave, for sojourners' behoof,
 in public made will be; and, since auspicious is  420
 this day, I fain would hear, at once, the God's reply.
 (*To* KREOUSA.) Around the altars, pious-wise, my lady, go,
 fresh Daphnê-branches bearing; pray to Gods that I
 of children hopeful presage bring from Pûthion halls!

KREOUSA,

 It shall, it shall be so!—(*She takes leave of* XOUTHOS *who, having
  dismissed his guards (who salute and retire by left parodos), enters the temple.*

KREOUSA, (*continuing*) *to audience.* For outrage criminal  425
 if Loxias even chose atonement due to make,
 he ne'er could prove himself, in all respects, my friend;
  (*With concentrated bitterness,*)
 but what he gives I can't refuse, for he's a God.

KREOUSA *dismisses her guards, who retire as above, and, accompanied by her
  two prospoloi, exit by left side scene gate.*

HIEROS, *solus, in meditation,*

 In such mysterious words, and terms of veil'd abuse,
 what prompts this foreign dame to oft our God traduce?  430
 Comes she to ask for oracles to serve a friend?
 No! Secret bound is she to keep what brings her here.—
 Anent Erektheus' daughter why concern myself?
 She's not affied to me; and now, 'tis time to fill
 the golden urns with holy water from the tank,  435
 and all the floors asperge. (*Exit* HIEROS *into the temple.*)

KORUPHAIOS *mounts the thymelè and addresses the audience.*

I can't forbear to blame

Lord Phoibos! What possesseth him to maids deflow'r,
desert the infants whom in private he begets,
and let them die? (*To statue*) Behave not thus; as strong thou art
and wise, be virtuous, too! (*To audience*) When mortals sins commit, 440
they always trenchant chastisement from Gods receive.
Then, who will say 'tis just that they, who've fram'd the laws
for us, of breach of right themselves should guilty be?

(*To the statues of the several Gods in the peristyle*)
Were ye (it ne'er can be, I merely put the case,)
adjudg'd by men the fines for rapes in cash to pay,                445
great Gods, Poseidôn, Phoibos, Zeus who rul'st the skies,
your temples' treasure-chambers soon would empty be!
To carnal joys inclin'd, in lieu of continence,
iniquitous ye are! The human race revile
no more! When we your acts nefarious list to ape,              450
we well may say, " We've learn'd our worst of crimes from you !"

(KORUPHAIOS *descends the thymelè.*)

*Ode* 3. *Khoros. Lyric.*
*Khoros kneels, and adores the statues of Athenê and Artemis, in the peristyle.*
*Full Khoros, in monotone.*                                 *Strophè.*

To thee, free from pangs of a birth,
Aneilcithuiê, we cry!

FIRST, KHOREUTES, *in monotone.*

Athênê, my ador'd, whom
Promêtheus Titânos educ'd                                    455
from Zeus, by stroke on his head
with a sharp weapon, hear me, my Nîcê,
to the Pûthïon hill, from
Olûmpos' gilded halls, in a flight
thro' the air, to the courts come,                           460

where Phoibos, who sitteth o'er
the entry to Earth, propounds,
from a beprais'd-by-the-Choirs Trĭpŏd, in
wise Oracle just Spells!—

*Second* KHOREUTES, *in monotone*,

Be nigh too, chaste Lêtŏgĕnês!—                                    465

*Full* KHOROS, *in monotone*,

As a Maid, as a Goddes' each,
ye Phoibos' pure, worshipp'd, blest sisters,
we beseech ye to beg, to pray
that a daughter of old Erek-
thëos hear, from a Spell, that a babe's to be her's!    470
One long she has wish'd for.—

*The* KHOROS *rises, and performs a pantomime, in the orchestra, during the following antistrophe, the* FIRST *and* SECOND KHOREUTES *not joining in any of the ballet movements.*

FIRST KHOREUTES, *to* KHOROS,                         *Antistrophè.*

    The prime source, dear friends, of a'sur'd
      bliss, 'mongst Humanity, springs
      from hale children.—A kind Fate
    the man's bless'd, who sees that his home's      475
      ancestral halls are alive
    with his healthy, his amiable young sons:
      to inherited wealth they
    gain, *their* sons, by Right, can a'tain,
      thus a race has a long line:                        480
    their Sire, when in woe, they soothe,
    through prosperous years befriend:
    menace if hosts from abroad the Land,
      their spears to her help flock.—

·⊦

SECOND KHOREUTES, *to audience,*

By far more than gold to acquire,     485
or of a king to become consort,
to nurse mine own dear infants *I'd* choose!
To be childles' a lot's abhorr'd,
be she blam'd who a'proves of it !—
By a limited wealth tho' my state be upheld,     490
Gods, bless me with offspring !—

*Here the* KHOROS *ceases to dance, and re-enters, by side-scene gate,* KREOUSA, *attended by her* PROSPOLOI, *and* THERAPES *of the temple, bearing, on their heads, baskets of laurel, with some of which* KREOUSA *ascends, and decorates the shrine of* PÀN.

FULL KHOROS, *with joined hands, dancing round the thymelè,*

Hail, ô Pân, thy sanctu'ry !   Hail     *Epôdè.*
thou steep rock, (nigh to Măkrai
  by cavities ypierc'd,)
where, in a dance, three children of old     495
  Agraulis disport on a green,
merrily, merrily, by Pallădon
  fam'd shrine, flutes who breathe
to vari'd hymns, in an oft-
chang'd mode, when a pipe-refrain     500
  trill'st thou forth, ô Pân,
seated in thy cav'd fane !—

*The* KHOROS, *here, ceases to dance.*

KREOUSA, *to audience, sadly,*

Where an unhappy girl carri'd a babe, ('twas her own
By God Phoibos,) laid it, too, prey to wild birds, for
beasts, on a prowl, a feast bloody—

KREOUSA *sinks, sobbing, on* PÀN'S *altar steps; her two* PROSPOLOI *run to her assistance.*

KORUPHAIOS, *to audience,*

               a shame t'a curs'd           505
union!  Where, in a tale, or on work of a loom,
can we find a case when a son of a God,
upon Earth, had a bright lot?

KREOUSA, *having reverently placed wreaths upon sundry altars, directs, by gestures, her two women to await the arrival of* XOUTHOS *from the temple; and, followed by the* THERAPES, *exit by side-scene gate. The* PROSPOLOI *remain on the stage, during the next interlude and succeeding scenes, until they join the* KHOROS *in the orchestra.*

*The curtain closes.  End of Episode.*

———— ——

*First Interlude.  Pageant and dumb show.  The curtain is withdrawn.*

*The festival procession issues from the temple, on its career round the town, previous to the " common sacrifice," which is about to take place " before the nave," after which oracles are to be proclaimed in public.*

*After a flourish of trumpets, enter, from the vestibule, sundry adult and juvenile therapes bearing censers, candelabra and urns of gold and silver, also images and attributes of Apollôn, under canopies : musicians with horns, trumpets and pipes : men and boy choristers : the five " hosioi," attended, and followed by priests and pages : the prophetess, followed by priestesses and virgins in a solemn dance : the " hieros," as " daphnephoros," attired as Apollôn-Movsagêtes, crowned with a wreath of laurel, a branch of which he carries in his right hand, and in his left a lyre ; the train of his " long robe " of cloth of gold is borne by pages ; from the right parodos, to the proscenium, arrives a gilded car, drawn by four white horses, abreast ; the " daphnephoros " ascends this vehicle, and stands therein.  The procession passes out, by the left parados, followed by a train of boys and girls in white dresses, and crowned with roses.  Amidst clouds of incense, accompanied by vocal and instrumental music, the pageant is continued until the curtain closes.*

*End of first interlude.*

## PROSODE.

*The curtain is withdrawn. Scene as before. Time, the first hour after noon. The two* PROSPOLOI *are seated on the temple steps. Enter, by side-scene gate,* HIEROS, *in his first costume, with bow and quiver.*

HIEROS, *to the* PROSPOLOI,                                        *Trochaic.*

    Prospŏloi, ye maids, who keeping constant watch, your lord await,    510
    seated near the temple's platform, whence the incense-clouds arise,
    say, hath left the trĭpŏd-apartment, sacred seat oracular,

                  *(here he makes reverence to the shrine,)*

    Xouthos, or, in hope of offspring, craving counsel still is he?
FIRST PROSPOLOS,
    Sir, he's there, within the cella; through those gates he's pass'd not out.—
SECOND PROSPOLOS,
    Hark! I hear a sound of closing doors, as if approach'd he now!    515
FIRST PROSPOLOS,
    Sure enough my royal master hast'ning forth thou may'st behold!

*(Enter, from the temple,* XOUTHOS, *running with extended arms towards* HIEROS, *who advances to meet him.)*

XOUTHOS, *to* HIEROS, *offering to embrace him,*
    Health to thee, my son! (*Aside*) This prologue, truth to speak, beseems me most!
HIEROS, *startled, and drawing back,*
    Well am I—an' keep'st thy senses, well 't will be for both of us.
XOUTHOS,
    Kiss thy hand to me in homage! Yield to mine embrace thy waist!
HIEROS,
    Has't thy wits, sir-stranger, maddens thee some angry God's despite?   520

XOUTHOS, *embracing* HIEROS,

 Could I sane be, if a lov'd one, newly found, I fail'd to kiss?

HIEROS, *raising his arms to guard his laurel crown,*

 Hold, for fear thy sacrilegious hand the Deity's wreath destroy!

XOUTHOS,

 Nought I'd spoil; I'd simply fondle darling just vouchsaf'd to me.

HIEROS, *breaking away,*

 Cease, I say! Wilt not release me ere an arrow pierce thy lungs?

XOUTHOS,

 Why should'st flee from *me?* Acknowledge him who chiefly claims thy love!525

HIEROS, *adjusting bow and arrow,*

 Choose not I to bandy words with silly, rash, or crazy guests.

XOUTHOS, *pathetically,*

 Slay and burn me, though, so doing, parricidal be thy crime!

HIEROS, *laughing and lowering his bow,*

 Thou, forsooth, my sire? My laughter should not that remark provoke?

XOUTHOS,

 No! Ensuing explanation soon will show what I'm to thee.

HIEROS,

 What would'st tell me?

XOUTHOS,

      I'm thy father, thou'rt my true and only son.    530

HIEROS,

 Who hath said so?

XOUTHOS,

      He who rear'd thee. Yes, my boy, 'twas Loxías.

HIEROS,

 Who's thy witness?

XOUTHOS,

      By the God's spell, in the temple 'twas declar'd.

HIEROS,

 Thou enigma heard'st misleading.

XOUTHOS,
>Heard not I a plain response ?

HIEROS,
>What were Phoibos' words ?

XOUTHOS,
>" To meet me he who first should chance to come "—

HIEROS,
>And on what occasion ?

XOUTHOS, *continuing,*
>Just as I should quit the God's abode— 535

HIEROS,
>What would hap to him who met thee ?

XOUTHOS, *continuing,*
>he my son should surely be.

HIEROS,
>Giv'n to thee, or thine begotten ?

XOUTHOS, *devoutly,*
>Giv'n was he whom I begot.

HIEROS,
>Were to me thy steps directed ?

XOUTHOS,
>Tow'rds none else, believe me, child

HIEROS, *in contemplation,*
>Whence arriv'd this chance ?

XOUTHOS,
>A marvel well may't seem to both of us.

HIEROS, *starting,*
>Eàh, but whom did'st make my mother ?

XOUTHOS,
>*That* I can't presume to say. 540

HIEROS, *disappointed,*
>Did not Phoibos say ?

XOUTHOS,
>In pleasure too absorb'd was I to ask.

HIEROS, *sarcastically,*
> Was't the Earth which gave me being?

XOUTHOS,-*simply,*
>> Ne'er did soil produce a babe.

HIEROS,
> How can I be thine?

XOUTHOS,
>> I know not, *that* I leave the God to prove.

HIEROS, *after some pause,*
> Prithee, let's discuss the subject!

XOUTHOS,
>> Well suggestest thou, my son.

HIEROS,
> Had'st thou e'er illicit union?

XOUTHOS,
>> Ay, in flush of giddy youth.                    545

HIEROS,
> Ere Erektheus' child thou wedded'st?

XOUTHOS,
>> Ne'er such 'venture, since, had I.

HIEROS.
> Fruit was I of that connection?

XOUTHOS,
>> Suits its date thine age, methinks.

HIEROS,
> How was I transported hither?

XOUTHOS,
>> How indeed? I fail to guess.

HIEROS,
> Trav'lling, too, so long a journey?

XOUTHOS,
>> *That* perplexing seems to me.

38

HIEROS, *after some pause,*
    Cam'st, ere now, to Pûthion mountain?
XOUTHOS,
                                Once.  At torch-feast Bakkhîon. 550
HIEROS,
    And the proxĕnos who hous'd thee.
XOUTHOS, *hesitating,*
                          'Mongst the Delphik women he—
HIEROS,
    " introduc'd " thee?  Would'st not say so?
XOUTHOS, *laughing,*
                            Bakkhos' Mainädes they were.
HIEROS, *shocked,*
    Sober was't, or warm'd by liquor?
XOUTHOS,
                        Steep'd in Bakkhos' wild delights.
HIEROS, *vexed,*
    Really, thus was I created?
XOUTHOS,
                  Fate hath led me tow'rds my son.
HIEROS,
    How arriv'd I 'fore this temple?
XOUTHOS,
                    Cast thee here the girl, perhaps.    555
HIEROS, *bitterly,*
    Hence I 'scap'd a slave's condition!
XOUTHOS,
                  Now accept a sire, my child!
HIEROS, *in contemplation,*
    'Tis not meet the Gods distrusting.
XOUTHOS,
                  Wisdom shows that sentiment.
HIEROS, *still in contemplation,*
    What by me should more be wish'd for—

XOUTHOS,

                          All in proper light thou view'st.

HIEROS, *continuing, with irony and incredulity,*

     than that mighty Zeus' own grandson—

XOUTHOS,

                          should be he who thee begot.

HIEROS, *to* XOUTHOS,

     Him may I caress who gat me?

XOUTHOS,

                          So shal't *thou* thy God obey.            560

HIEROS, *kissing his own hand, prostrating himself, and embracing* XOUTHOS' *knees,*

     Sire, accept my homage!

XOUTHOS, *embracing and raising* HIEROS,

                    Pleas'd am I such filial speech to hear.

HIEROS,

     This indeed 's a day auspicious!

XOUTHOS,

                          Sweet content it brings to me.

HIEROS, *in contemplation,*

     Ne'er may I, mine absent mother, chance thy form to gaze upon?

     Now I long to, more than ever, view thy face, whoe'er thou art!

     But, perhaps, thou'rt dead and buri'd! Hence, such joy may ne'er be mine. 565

*Full* KHOROS, *to* XOUTHOS,                                    *Iambic.*

     That signal luck befalls thy house we all rejoice,

     but hope that queen Kreousa yet may bear a child,

     and long continued be Erektheus' noble line.

XOUTHOS, *to* HIEROS,

     O son, that I should light on thee, in mercy, God's

     ordain'd! My joy it is to fold thee in my arms,            570

     and gainest thou, unlook'd for, what most precious is.—

     As ardent wish ha'st thou, so ardent wish have I;

     thy long-lost mother's person thy desire's to see,

     and mine's the style of her who gave thee birth to know;

     we may, in course of time, find both fulfill'd, perhaps.—

Resign thy post precarious, quit this God's demesne,
to gay Athênaī come, a parent gratify ;
thy father's royal sceptre, there, and boundless wealth
await thee, boy, and not ill-happ'd in two respects,
not lowly born, nor poor in means shal't *thou* be deem'd,                580
for rank and rich emoluments shall swell thy state !—

(*Observing* HIEROS *absorbed in thought.*)
Why silent art ?   Thine eyes why castest tow'rds the ground ?
What cares oppress thy heart ?   Ah, why from sprightly mien
such startling change, which smites thy sire with sudden awe ?

HIEROS, *having mounted the altar steps, to* XOUTHOS,
We know that ev'ry distant object we behold                                585
an aspect different presents, when closely view'd.—
Enraptur'd though I hail th' unlook'd for happy chance
which leads a father tow'rds me, hark to what my mind
is brooding on !—Athênaī's race is said to be
earth-born, by alien new connections undefil'd ;                           590
in me 'twill see a youth with double stain besmirch'd,
from foreign parent sprung, of spurious birth declar'd ;
thus stigmatiz'd, and void of public influence,
consider'd I shall be as one of no account :
within its town's first ranks if I obtrude myself,                         595
to occupy a place, all those who needy be
will hate me much, their due precedence loth to yield :
of those, whom ample means, assur'd, permit to rest
in placid, stately guise, exempt from worldly cares,
I shall, with folly charg'd, incur the ridicule,                          600
unless amid the city's din I dwell retir'd :
if I, amongst the chiefs who o'er the burgh preside,
aspire to honour's post, by all who suffrage own
my claims will challeng'd be, for is't not true, my prince,
that foremost men, who hold a nation's dignities,                          605

to enterprizing rivals hostile front oppose ?—
If I, a stranger, come beneath thy roof to bide,
thy hapless wife, denied an offspring, who so long
hath shar'd thy fortunes good and evil, left alone
to face Despair, her dreary Fate will more bewail.                           610
And, would there not be cause why *me* she should detest ?
Ay, since no son she hath, on thine she'd sourly gaze,
on special step at thy throne's foot if stand should he.—
So, either wilt thou cast me off, to please thy spouse,
or favour me, and summon Discord tow'rds thy dome.—                          615
What modes to slay, with knives, or poison'd philtre-cups,
have women not devis'd who've wish'd their lords' demise ?
Good sooth, dear sir, I pity much thy dame, in age
advancing, childless !   Lot too sad, too hard to bear,
hath queen of noble stock by barren womb accurs'd.—                          620
They err who deem that regal state delightsome is ;
while strikes the sight its pomp, o'er all its palace halls
a gloom must lour, for how can blest be counted he
who, shudd'ring aye from fear, expecting violence,
drags through Life's span ?   In private station rather I                    625
would spend my days in peace, than be some mighty king,
who looks for social glee from worthless parasites,
who virtuous folk mislikes, and dreads untimely Death.—
Thou'lt say, perchance, that " gold all ills can neutralize,
" for wealth all joys procures ; " I'd ne'er endure the coil                 630
which treasure-hoards entail ; I shun what plagues the brain :
may mod'rate means be mine, and no solicitude !—
Of course serene, till now pursu'd, vouchsafe to hear !—
The prime of blessings all I've had, a term of ease
apart from bustling crowds ; no wight importunate                            635
disturb'd my way's smooth tenour ; vantage-ground to cede
to those of lower grade 's a trial most severe.—
'Mid pray'rs to Gods my service past, and cheery chat

with people ever gay, for here's no sign of woe :
departing guests I sped, and welcom'd those who came,                640
as new and pleasant they to me as I to them.—
What mortals most should pray for, e'en against their wills,
is hap like mine; for Law and Nature's bent alike
have made me this God's serf !—

(*He kneels and adores Phoibos' statue, then descends and makes respectful reverence to*
   XOUTHOS),
                              While musing thus, methinks,
'twere better here to stay than join thy court, my sire;             645
so, leave me where I am !   Content affords a bliss
as sweet, in sphere confin'd, as one which boundless is.—

KORUPHAIOS, *to* HIEROS,
   Discreetly has't thou preach'd.   Would that so fortunate
   some friends of mine had been as thy discourse t'have heard !

XOUTHOS, *to* HIEROS, *whose homily he has heard with impatience,*
   Forbear such talk !   Thy rare good fortune learn to prize !—     650
   Here, where I've haply found thee, boy, my purpose is
   the primal sacrifice for thy " genèthliă "
   to celebrate, and hold a common-table-feast ;
   for thee, as new-come guest, with banquets I'll delight,
   and straightway guide thee tow'rds Athênai's lordly land,         655
   as if no son of mine, but visitant, thou wer't.—
   Though thee t'agnize in public would rejoice my heart,
   to make my childless consort envious wish not I.
   Occasion soon I'll seek to influence her will
   to leave to thee the sceptre wielded now by me.—                  660
   " Iôn " thy name shall be, to note thy lucky chance ;
   as " coming," first, to meet me " coming " from the nave,
   the " Coming Man " art thou !   Be thine to invite thy friends ;
   at supper bid them all, in loving speech, adieu,
   the sacred Delphik city soon about to quit !—                     665

*(To the* PROSPOLOI *on the stage, and to the* KHOROS,)*

Now, list to me, ye waiting maids ! If aught ye tell
my wife of what ye've heard, I'll doom ye all to Death !—

*(To* HIEROS)

Come, let's depart !

HIEROS, *henceforth to be styled* IÔN,

    " Good Fortune " halts in one " respect " :
unless I find the woman, sire, who gave me birth,
my life a blank must be.—I'd pray, could pray'rs avail,    670
that she who bore me might to Atthis' race belong,
that I, in public, might harangue by right of her's ;
for alien men in charter'd boroughs domicil'd,
though citizens by writ, must like to slaves be mute,
since they of open speech no licens'd freedom own.—    675

*Exeunt* XOUTHOS *and* IÔN *by left side-scene gate.*

*The* PROSPOLOI, *awaiting* KREOUSA'S *return, saunter about the colonnades, and are
seen to converse with therapes and priestesses who pass to and fro.*

ODE 4. KHOROS. LYRIC.

*Full* KHOROS, *to audience,*              *Strophè.*

   Be sure tears, in a terrible gush, *must* be shed ;
   high pitch'd wails of angry woe *must* arise,
    when our ador'd tŭrannos hears how the king
     lit on a son, to-day,
while *she*, denied all babes, a hopeles' wife remains !—    680

    FIRST KHOREUTES, *to* PHOIBOS' *statue,*

But, ô seer, produc'd by Lêtô, in what strict sense spoke thy rede ?
  How did he come, the boy, who here, 'midst thy courts,
    bred as an orphan was ? Denote his mother !
     *I'll* not thy spell thus render ; a    685
     play on a phrase is it ?

FULL KHOROS.

Scares us this new event;
how wil'it, oh, how wil'it end?

SECOND KHOREUTES, *to* KHOROS,

Thoro'ly, thoro'ly strange, verily, 'tis to hear     690
sanction a blest God's spell
success, by fraud, achiev'd by one,
through veins of whom blood alien wells!
Be sure that all with me'll agree!

FIRST KHOREUTES, *to* KHOROS,         *Antistrophè.*

My friends, are we to tell our mistres' what we     695
have heard, that he's a false guilty spouse,
he who was all in all to *her*, hope of whose
ever was hers?

SECOND KHOREUTES, *to* KHOROS.

Poor dame!
Though *he'll* be blithe, *she's* bound to fade, by griefs decay'd;     700
verily prematurely grey grown, never again be lov'd by *him*.

FIRST HEMIKHOROS.

Pitiful wretch!   A houseles' waif gains a home;
then, at a peaceful hearth, he turns bliss to woe!

SECOND HEMIKHOROS.

A'curs'd, a'curs'd be *he* who wrongs
her we so much respect!

FIRST KHOREUTES *to the statues in the peristyle,*

Ne'er let *him* 'mongst pyres alight,     705
induc'd by a fav'rable omen,
offer ye cakes, my Gods!

SECOND KHOREUTES, *to* KHOROS.

Be, tho', my queen a'sur'd
[her friend that *I'll* prove thro'
my life!   For any King's sole sway,
by right defin'd, she wots]                               710
a champion warm am I.

*(The* KHOROS, *having made reverence to the statue of* BAKKHOS, *in the peristyle, with joined hands dances round the thymelè.)*

FULL KHOROS.                                              *Epôdê.*

E'en now to feast wends this new-found
son, while the sire, tho' just a'riv'd,
in haste seeks thy crags, Pàrnèsos sublime,
thy steep, rough precipice, also thy seat, where oft,   715
to a melody, Bakkhĭos wav'st thou thy torch, bound, too, ·
those nimble feet 'mid Mainădes all, in a gay night-dance!

*Here the dance ceases, and the* KHOROS *kneels.*

*Full* KHOROS, *in monotone, to* BAKKHOS' *statue,*

Ne'er let our own belov'd city a'proach the lad!
A stark corpse be *he*, ere we espy the dawn!          720

KORUPHAIOS, *sarcastically, to* KHOROS,
   " City " beset can well hit on a fair pretext
      *alien aid* to seek !

KHOROS, *rising, angrily,*
   Enough had we al' of it whilst rul'd the land
      Erektheus, the king!

*Enter, from side-scene gate, in changed mask,* KREOUSA, *who has now made the round of the altars, and enter, at the same moment, from the left parodos,* PRESBUS *walking with difficulty, leaning on his staff :* KREOUSA *advances to meet him.*

KREOUSA, *to* PRESBUS,                                   *Iambic.*
   Presbûs, my sire Erektheus' paidagôgos, who          725

was't, through his life, his tried and trusty servitor,
uprouse thyself to learn what this God's voice declar'd,
that thou may'st share my joy, if Loxias, the prince,
hath told my spouse that children soon shall grace our hearths!—
If fortunate we be, 'tis sweet our friends to meet,     730
and, if Mischance befall us, (such may Gods avert!)
consoling 'tis the eyes of genial folk to view.—     .

(PRESBUS *kneels, and kisses the hand of* KREOUSA, *who raises and embraces him*),

    I'll always watch o'er thee, as thou did'st o'er my sire,
    and, though thy queen and mistress, treat thee like a sire.

PRESBUS, *to* KREOUSA,

    My child, thy worthy parents' worthy sentiments     735
    preserv'st thou well; no-wise debasest thou the names
    of noble ancestors whose source upsprung from earth:
    but help me, help me tow'rds the temple, lead me there,
    for arduous seems the stair-ascent; assist my limbs,
    physician-like, thy care afford me worn by age!     740

KREOUSA,

    Then follow me, and how thou tak'st thy steps beware!

PRESBUS, *endeavouring to move briskly*,

    Behold!
    Though sluggish be my feet, my spirit's lively still.

KREOUSA,

    But firmly plant thy staff, for slopeth here the ground!

PRESBUS,

    Nought sees my wand, and these old eyes but dimly gaze.

KREOUSA, *taking* PRESBUS *by the hand*,

    Relax not thou thine efforts, though thy words be true!
        745

PRESBUS,

    Perchoice I'd not so do, but strength my body needs.—

*(He stumbles, and falls upon the temple steps. The two PROSPOLOI advance from the colonnades and, having made reverence to KREOUSA, hasten to PRESBUS' assistance.)*

KREOUSA, *to the* PROSPOLOI,
>Ye, women, who with loom and distaff serve me well,
>anent his journey's object say what fortune hath
>my lord experienc'd! Shall babes be born to us?
>Respond, for if propitious be the news ye bring,      750
>on no ungracious mistress pleasure ye'll bestow!

FIRST PROSPOLOS, *wailing,*
>Iô, Daimôn!

KREOUSA,
>Thy speech's prelude augurs not success assur'd.

FIRST PROSPOLOS, *wailing,*
>Iô! Poor wretch!

PRESBUS, *to* PROSPOLOI,
>Is cause for grief from oracles our lord's receiv'd?      755

SECOND PROSPOLOS, *to* FIRST *about to speak,*
>Hold! Why commit an act inducing speedy death?

KREOUSA,
>What means this dismal chant? Of whom afraid are ye?

FIRST PROSPOLOS,
>Oh, how to speak, or how be silent, how to act?

KREOUSA,
>Speak out! At some mischance of mine ye seem to hint.

FIRST PROSPOLOS,
>I'll tell thee, ay would I, though twice 'twere mine to die!      760
>
>*(Slowly and sympathetically,)*
>
>'Tis not for thee, my queen, thine infants 'tween thy arms
>to clasp, and next thy bosom press their tiny lips!

6

*Ode 5. Monostrophica—Lyric.*

KREOUSA, *shrieking,*                                                      *Strophè* 1.

    O Death, receive me !

PRESBUS,

    Daughter, we——

KREOUSA, *wailing,*

        Sad's my lot ; for years borne have I

    misery, tacitly !   'Twas a terrible load, my friends !

PRESBUS,

    Alas, my girl, we lost are !                                765

KREOUSA,

        Aî, aî ! Aî, aî !   A sharp pang of ago-

    ny, in a spasm, has yerk'd to pierce through my lungs !

PRESBUS,

    Wail not, belov'd dame——

KREOUSA,

        What's to restrain my laments ?

PRESBUS, *continuing,*

    til' we're a'pris'd if——                                    770

KREOUSA,

        Aught be dispatch'd to my inn ?

PRESBUS, *continuing,*                                                     *Iambic.*

    if share thy husband all thy grief for such mishap,

    if whelm'd he be by woe, or if thou weep'st alone.

FIRST PROSPOLOS, *to* PRESBUS,                                             *Lyric.*

    Hear then, my man, a son to him how Loxîas

    presented, as a boon, whom the queen's not claim upon!

                                           775

KREOUSA, *wailing,*                                                        *Strophè* 2.

        What ye have added is a crown to misery !

        This is a dolour, an ill to mourn !

PRESBUS, *to* PROSPOLOS,

    Is he to be soon got ?   Through what woman ?   Is the young

    child born, of whom thou talk'st ?   How spake the oracle ?

FIRST PROSPOLOS, *to* KREOUSA,                                                              *Iambic.*

   E'en now a bloomy, nobly form'd, egregious youth                    780
   receiv'd thy spouse from Loxīas, before my eyes.

KREOUSA, *to* PROSPOLOS,                                              *Lyric—Strophè* 3.

   What say'st? Oh, 'tis a horrible, nefarious tale which ye relate to me!

PRESBUS, *to* PROSPOLOS,                                                              *Iambic.*

   Methinks so, too. How clos'd the charge oracular?                    785
   Describe what happ'd! Speak clearly! Tell us, who's the lad?

FIRST PROSPOLOS, *to* KREOUSA,

   The God declar'd he'd " give thy spouse a son in him
   " whom first (the fane when leaving,) chance should he to meet."

KREOUSA, *wailing*,                                                                    *Lyric.*

       O tŏ tŏ toî! Oh what a
  misery, misery, oh what an agony, what an agony, to be doom'd to pine, 790
    aye alone, at home, sans offspring!

PRESBUS, *to* PROSPOLOS,

   Who stands elect? Who first appear'd before the spouse
   of our aggriev'd queen? Saw he where, or how, the boy?

FIRST PROSPOLOS, *to* KREOUSA,                                                        *Iambic.*

   Can'st, my respected lady, call to mind the youth
   who'd swept the temple floors? I tell thee he's the son.          795

KREOUSA, *wailing*,                                                          *Lyric—Epôdê.*

     Oh, would that I might waft,
  airily, through space, far b'yond Hellêniên land, to the Hespĕròn
   starry realm, so sharp's the agony, my friends!

PRESBUS, *to* PROSPOLOS,                                                              *Iambic.*

   And what's the name by which the father calls the son?
   Do'st know? Is't undetermin'd? Kept a secret is't?                    800

FIRST PROSPOLOS, *to* PRESBUS,

   " Iôn," as " coming," first of all, to meet the Sire.

PRESBUS,

   And how's the mother styl'd?

FIRST PROSPOLOS,

   I cannot say; the king    ·
hath gone to bespeak his son's " genèthlion " feast within
the holy tents, bid guests, and sacrifice to Gods,     805
but kept the queen in ignorance of these designs.—
And now, old man, thou ha'st the sum of all my news.

*The* PROSPOLOI, *having received congé from their queen, retire by left parodos,*
 *and reappear in the orchestra.* KREOUSA *continues to lament.  A pause.*

PRESBUS, *to* KREOUSA,

   A traitor is thy spouse, my patroness; thy grief,
thy wrongs are shar'd by me; his heartless, guilty wiles
have harm'd us both.  From King Erektheus' realm, belike,   810
shall we be driv'n.—'Tis not the hate I bear thy lord,
but tender love for thee which prompts me thus to speak:
he wedded thee who march'd a stranger through thy town,
enjoy'd thy wide estates and all thy heritage,
yet, prov'd it is, on concubines he's slily been    815
begetting sons.—I'll say how " slily " he's behav'd.—
When barren he perceiv'd thee, not content to bow
to lot like thine, in thy distress to sympathize,
he " slily " hir'd a leman slave his couch to share;
a boy she gave him, whom he sent abroad to friends   820
at Delphoi, there to th' God devoted, nurs'd to be,
brought up in strict seclusion, nameless, 'midst his halls.
Soon as he finds a ripe " ephèbos " grown the babe,
to pray for offspring, there, persuades he thee to go.—
The God 's disclos'd the truth, and Xouthos' fraud 's reveal'd;  825
while rear'd was here his bairn, two schemes did he devise;
if he detected were, the child to Phoibos he'd
resign; if undetected, 'gainst contingencies
to guard, intrigue would he to make his brat the king.—

*(Laughing scornfully,)*

Appropriate agnomen, novel too, he forg'd ;                    830
  the lad who tow'rds him came the " coming man " he calls.—

KREOUSA, *wailing,*

  Ah me !

KORUPHAIOS, *to audience,*

    How much those evil-doers I detest
  who criminal schemes conceive, and try to gloss them o'er
  with guile sophistical !   I'd rather choose my friends
  'mongst honest simple carles, than rogues, however wise.         835

PRESBUS, *to* KREOUSA,

    Of degradations all can'st *thou* endure the worst ?
  Can'st lead, as master, tow'rds thy hearth a casteless waif,
  whose mother's some impure, abandon'd, lowly slave ?—
  If child from noble woman born he'd hous'd beneath
  thy roof, (had'st been assur'd thou ne'er could'st issue have,)      840
  less scandal had there been ; had'st scouted such idea,
  'mongst Aiŏlos' young brood should sought have been an heir.—
  Be thine to act an injur'd female's part !   Prepare,
  by whetting blades, by exercising subtle sleights,
  or mixing pois'nous drugs, to slay thy crafty mate,               845
  his stripling too, ere they thy murderers become !
  Ay, if thou spar'st their lives, expect to lose thy own !
  When, in the same abode, two mutual foes reside,
  to one the vantage ground needs must the other yield.—
  Revenge thy duty is ; depend on me for help !—                    850
  Be mine to wend within the festal tent to kill
  the youth, and thus, alive or dead, (I may be slain,)
  my debt for bed and board my patrons kind repay !—

KORUPHAIOS, *to audience,*

  'Tis but the name of "slave" which humble wights degrades ;
  in all respects besides, no men of free descent                  855
  a whit superior are to serfs of worthy fame.

FIRST KHOREUTES, *to* KREOUSA.

    And I, with thee, my dearest lady, wish to share
a common grief   if not to nobly live, to die !—

*Ode* 6.   *Monôdê*.   *Lyric.*

KREOUSA, *in contemplation,*

        How, Heart, can rest I speech-bound ?
        How tell such a tale of an union's           860
        black guilt ?   How's Shame to be cast off,
      for what else cou'd avail as curb to my tongue ?
      *Me* for a loose act who on earth can a'raign ?—
           (*Here her agitation increases.*)
    False to thy wife, ar't thou, my spouse, not a wretch ?—
        Of a child chance lost, of a home joy's fled !     865
      Gone's last gleam of a hope to retain fame
      unsulli'd, as all *must* be reveal'd now,
           connection abhorr'd,
      and birth of a babe, a bewail'd babe !
  (*Here she extends her arms towards the peristyle statues.*)
        I swear tho', by Zeus, by the starry domain,    870
        and her, the ador'd one, a guard to my rocks,
        likewise the rever'd Trítônïădên
          many-flow'rd lake's shore,
      not to keep that " guilt " any more conceal'd ;
    of a load let, at once, this breast be reliev'd !     875
           (*To the Khoros,*)
    Hot tears, in a flood, run adown fro' my eyes,
    through grief when come to my mind gross wrongs
    from puissant God first, next from a man.—
          Hear me denounce each
    ill-doer who reproach to my couch brought !—    880
      (*Here she addressess* PHOIBOS' *statue.*)
    *Thou,* for strains from lyre with sev'n strings,

so renown'd thro' the world, *thou* who, skill'd in
   melody, to rustics ton'st, sans breath,
*(Here she indicates the yoke of the lyre on the statue's pedestal.)*
   those horns, chanting hymns 'mongst Mousai,
      blame reach *thee*, ô Lêtô's son,        885
      'fore this day-light cite I *thee !*
       *(Here she ascends the altar steps.)*
   Glitt'ring, *thou*, bright with gold-like
     locks, glided'st tow'rds me gath'ring,
   busily, krŏkŏsĕs yellow (which I i' my
     lap threw) for frocks' gold-ey'd gauds.—     890
Straightway grasping *these* bar'd wrists, and
   *me* dragging tow'rds dark grottoes,
   (" o Maiê, Maiê, help," I shriek'd,)
   *(Here she covers her mask with her hands.)*
God who the hearths despoils't, homage (a crime fraught rite,
     verily,) thou paid'st Kupris !        895
     *(Here is a pause, during which she sobs.)*
   Ill-starr'd girl, I bore that boy
   whom (I fear'd so my mother,)
   I plac'd where *me* thou laid'st with,
  (in a cave,) when adown, in a fright, in a swoon,    900
     sans sense, fell *I*, lorn victim !—
   Woe's me, he's gone, he's perish'd,
   (wild birds' feast, sunder'd piece-meal,)
     mine and thine ; poor babe !
*Thou* tho', to thy lute, no less sing'st res'nant paiáns !—    905
     *(Here she elevates her voice.)*
   Hôlá ! I'll call thee, Lêtô's
   son, mankind's destin'd
  lots' seer, the grand Lord on
  gold throne Earth's entrance gates before,
   hear, hear high-pitch'd voice cite thee !    910

Iô,
lecher ill-fam'd, who 's
this brat o' my spouse maintain'd long,
(not a doit tho' he gave
*thee*,) rear'd, cloth'd, hous'd 'midst Delphoi,                                   915
tho' my child, tho' thy *own* child, lost by neglect,
(fierce vultures' prey,) died, of a robe,
wrapp'd by a mother, in haste, round him, stripp'd !—
(*Furiously, and with scornful gesture,*)
Dêlos loathes thee, and loathes the bay's
foliage, which grows by the feathery palm,                                   920
since it was held in her hands by the Deity
Lêtô, who gave thee thy birth there !—

(KREOUSA *descends the altar steps, sobbing hysterically.*)

KORUPHAIOS, *to audience,*                                   *Iambic.*
Ah me, what ample store of woes is here detail'd !
Such mournful ditty hearing, who could choose but weep ?—

PRESBUS, *as if somewhat deaf, advances towards* KREOUSA.

PRESBUS, *to* KREOUSA,
As I survey thy face, my heart with pity swells,                                   925
my daughter dear ! Alack, my brain begins to turn !—
As some sea-skiff, while stemming waves which shock the prow,
is overwhelm'd by billows rushing o'er the stern,
so we, while stagg'ring 'neath Misfortune's heavy blow,
are fell'd by news of grievous ills we knew not of !—                                   930
What words were thine ? What charge 'gainst Loxias ha'st to bring ?
What bantling ha'st conceiv'd, and near what town depos'd,
to bestial maws devoted ?   Recommence thy plaints !

KREOUSA,
I must ; 'fore thee, old man, to do so though abash'd.

PRESBUS,
With those I love I've learn'd to kindly sympathize.                                   935

KREOUSA,

    Then hear the truth! Amongst Cĕkrôp's steep rocks thou know'st
    those northern crags, by all our people styl'd Mäkrai?

PRESBUS,

    The cliffs which Pån's recess and altar sanctify?

KREOUSA,

    Adventure dreadful there encounter'd I, alas!

PRESBUS,

    What was 't? Ere tell'st thy tale, my tears prepare to flow.     940

KREOUSA,

    There Phoibos had with me connection, 'gainst my will.

PRESBUS,

    Ah, girl, was that the cause of what I once descri'd?

KREOUSA,

    When mean'st? I'll answer, if thy shaft hath hit the mark.

PRESBUS,

    When thou that sickness had'st, whose source was known to none?

KREOUSA,

    It was; that nausea's reason 's now within thy ken.     945

PRESBUS,

    And how with Lord Apollôn union could'st thou hide?

KREOUSA,

    With patience hear my rede, old man! I bore a boy.

PRESBUS,

    When? Who deliver'd thee? Did'st travail quite alone?

KREOUSA,

    Alone; and tow'rds a cave where I that union had——

PRESBUS, *interrupting*,

    Then, where 's thy nursling? Never say thou childless ar't!     950

KREOUSA,

    He died, my friend; a prey for brutes laid out was he.

PRESBUS,

    He died? So base was Loxias? Had'st no aid from him?

7

KREOUSA,

    No jot.   My son in Haidês' mansion spends his youth.

PRESBUS,

    And who expos'd him thus ?   'Twas surely not thyself?

KREOUSA,

    It was.   Though dim the light, in shawls I swath'd him well.      955

PRESBUS,

    Were none aware that thou deserted'st thus thy birth?

KREOUSA,

    None but the Gods of Evil-chance and Secrecy.

PRESBUS,

    Oh, how could'st bear to leave thy babe, in caves, alone ?

KREOUSA,

    Ah, how indeed ?   In doleful moans my voice arose.

PRESBUS, *sighing*,

    Phew !

    Both bold and hard was't thou, but harder still the God !      960

KREOUSA,

    Ay, had'st thou seen the child extend his hands to me——

PRESBUS,

    Sought he thy breast, or warm caress between thy arms ?

KREOUSA, *pressing her hands upon her bosom*,

    No doubt he long'd for *these*, 'gainst Nature's law withheld.

PRESBUS,

    Whence came to thee th' idea of casting off thy bairn ?

KREOUSA, *bitterly*,

    I thought the God would save the infant he begot.      965

PRESBUS, *weeping, and covering his mask with his mantle*,

    Ah me !   What wintry storms thy homestead's bliss have wreck'd !

KREOUSA,

    Oh, why, old man, do'st shed those tears, why hid'st thy face ?

PRESBUS,

    Thy luckless fate and thy lost Sire's I think upon.

KREOUSA, *sobbing*,
>Whate'er they love must mortals lose! Nought lasteth here.

PRESBUS,
>No more be ours, my dear, to utter vain laments!                   970

KREOUSA,
>What should I do? From hostile Fate no 'scape have we.

PRESBUS,
>First, wreak upon the God, who 's outrag'd thee, revenge!

KREOUSA,
>Can I, a mortal, subjugate the might supreme?

PRESBUS,
>Burn down Apollôn's sacred seat oracular!

KREOUSA,
>Such feat would Fear preclude. I'm too unnerv'd by Grief.            975

PRESBUS,
>But dare to use what grasp thou can'st, and kill thy spouse!

KREOUSA,
>Our nuptial tie I honour; faithful once was he.

PRESBUS,
>At least, the knave he seeks to palm on thee destroy!

KREOUSA,
>But how? The will to do so, not the pow'r, have I.

PRESBUS,
>To draw their swords and smite him bid thy body-guards!             980

KREOUSA,
>Let 's go and charge them so! Where should the deed be done?

PRESBUS,
>Where friends regaleth he, within the holy courts.

KREOUSA,
>For open onslaught far too weak 's my retinue.

PRESBUS,
>Ah me! Thy courage fails thee! Other course propose!

KREOUSA,

    Now, know I 've schemes conceiv'd; I 've means to work my will! 985

PRESBUS,

    In counsel, action too, accept my hearty aid!

KREOUSA,

    Then list! Thou'st heard of wars by Gaia's progeny?

PRESBUS,

    I 've learn'd Gigantes fought with Gods at fam'd Phlĕgrai.

KREOUSA,

    Where Gaiă bore the Gorgôn; monster dire she was.

PRESBUS,

    Her children's fellow combatant, to plague the Gods. 990

KREOUSA,

    Just so; and Zeus' wise daughter, Pallas, spear'd the beast.

PRESBUS,

    What outward form of savage animal was her's?

KREOUSA,

    With wreaths of vipers coil'd her scaly breast was arm'd.

PRESBUS,

    From thence arose the legend, taught me long ago—

KREOUSA,

    That chaste Athênê o'er her bosom wears the hide? 995

PRESBUS,

    Is 't Pallas' coat of mail, and " Aîgis " styl'd is it?

KREOUSA,

    So nam'd amid the Gods' battalions when she came.

PRESBUS,

    What hath this myth to do with plots to harm thy foes?

KREOUSA,

    Erïkthŏnios thou mind'st—old man, ha'st mem'ry lost?

PRESBUS,

    No, no, thine Earth-produc'd first ancestor was he. 1000

KREOUSA, *hesitating*,

    The Goddess, Pallas, sent to him, when newly born——

PRESBUS,

    What object?   Falter not, for much thou ha'st to tell!

KREOUSA,

    Two gouts of butcher'd Gorgôn's blood, the first which ooz'd.

PRESBUS,

    Upon the human system what effect to have?

KREOUSA,

    Twofold; one causes death, the other cures disease.        1005

PRESBUS,

    In what was plac'd the gift about the baby girt?

KREOUSA,

    Two golden belts; in them my father wore the charm.

PRESBUS,

    And thou the precious heir-loom gain'dst, on his demise?

KREOUSA, *indicating her bracelet*,

    Ay, Presbus, see the relic clasp'd around my wrist!

PRESBUS,

    How acts, respective-wise, the Deity's double boon?        1010

KREOUSA,

    The first gore-splash which shed the creature's hollow vein——

PRESBUS,

    How is 't appli'd to be?   What virtue dwells in it?

KREOUSA,

    A life-elixir 'tis, for maladies all it heals.

PRESBUS,

    What doth the second clot, of which thou lately spak'st?

KREOUSA,

    It slays; it flow'd from out the Gorgôn's snaky folds.        1015

PRESBUS,

    In common socket hold'st, or keep'st apart, the drops?

KREOUSA,
> Apart; for Good and Bad asunder must abide.

PRESBUS,
> My honour'd daughter, all which needful be thou ha'st!

KREOUSA, *indicating one of the rings of her bangle-like bracelet,*
> By this the boy shall die, and thou shal't poison him!

PRESBUS,
> Where? How employ'd? Be thine the order, mine the risk! 1020

KREOUSA,
> In our Athênai, on his journey tow'rds my house.

PRESBUS,
> Unwise I find thy speech. It seems thou spurn'st my plans.

KREOUSA,
> Say, ha'st, ere now, surmis'd what just hath struck my thoughts?

PRESBUS,
> An kill'st or not the lad, suspected wilt thou be!

KREOUSA,
> Thou 'rt right, for "stepdames hate all children," so they say. 1025

PRESBUS,
> Thou may'st the crime deny, if murder'd here he be!

KREOUSA,
> A pleasure 'tis to think that soon he may be so.

PRESBUS,
> Thy husband secrets keeps from thee, keep thine from him!

KREOUSA,
> Can'st guess what 's thine to do? When thou from me receiv'st
> the antique golden vase, which Pallas sent of yore, 1030
> haste where the solemn banquet slily holds my spouse,
> and, when the guests from feasting cease, and all prepare
> to offer Gods libations, draw 't from 'neath thy robe,
> and pour its fell contents amid the drink of him
> who hopes to lord it o'er my halls; and, if the youth 1035
> adown his throat the potion drain, ne'er view shall he

Athênê's glorious town, but here defunct remain.—
Take heed to hand th' envenom'd draught to none but him !

PRESBUS,

    Then, tow'rds the hostel's shelter, lady, bend thy steps,
    for I 'll this peril-fraught appointed task achieve !—        1040
    Bestir yourselves, my way-worn feet, be young again
    in work, however old in years, i'faith, ye be,
    and bear me swiftly on, enabling me to crush,
    and bar from our domains an heir my queen detests !

*Exeunt* KREOUSA *and* PRESBUS *by left parodos.*

KORUPHAIOS, *to audience,*

    For those who, blest by Fate, can passions angry tame        1045
    'tis well to pious precepts preach !   No holy Law
    will e'er restrain a man who means to slay a foe !—

*Here twilight is to be supposed to deepen to night, and the moon to rise. The* KHOROS,
*divided into two columns, kneels on each side of the thymelē, and adores the statue
of Kora in the peristyle.*

Ode 7.                 KHOROS.              *Lyric.*

FIRST HEMIKHOROS, *in monotone,*              *Strophè* 1.

    Einŏdïē (who protect'st each pilgrim all night,)
    Maiă's elect, triple-form'd, rever'd child,
    guard the poison (i'mix'd, to-day,) in th' ew'r, for a death    1050
    prepar'd well (Gorgôn's blood, which once that hell-fiend
        shed as a venom, it holds,) by my dear
        mistress sent to destroy a knave, an upstart,    1055
            who 'midst Erektheus' halls
            aspires, at once, to be hous'd !

SECOND HEMIKHOROS, *in monotone,*

    Ne'er let a stranger youth, sprung fro' new stock, in a land of ours reign !
        Our liege-lord be of old Erektheus' seed !
                         1060

KHOROS *rises.*

FIRST HEMIKHOROS, *to audience,*                   *Antistrophè* 1.

*Should* be by chance, by neglect, baulk'd hopes we build on,
   *should* in her able design the queen fail,
  *should* the wine by the boy be quaff'd not, straight by a sword,
  else cord round her throat, she wou'd wildly seek Death;       1065
     agony agony sharp succeeding,
    soon, soon *would* she, below, co'mence a new life!

SECOND HEMIKHOROS, *to audience,*

        Mark all! A dame, who can well
        lay claim to noble descent,         1070
life as a burthen holds, longs to die when she descries a bold chief,
    some base alien, a'sume her *own* state-rule!

*Here* KHOROS, *with joined hands, dances round the thymĕlĕ.*

FIRST KHOREUTES, *to audience, alluding to* BAKKHOS,     *Strophè* 2.

    Foul shame be that God's who a song loves,
    as he sits by the Khallïkhŏrossŏn well-side,—     1075

SECOND KHOREUTES, *alluding to* IÔN,

     should such a wretch behold the Eíkădôn
     torch alight,—

FIRST KHOREUTES, *continuing, alluding to* BAKKHOS,

        for nightly a vigil he keeps,
     at a time when on high thy stars, Zeus,
     (which in an airy dance whirl,
       a dance led by Selênê),     1080
       and Nêreus' fifty marine
     nymphs (who by sea, who by river,
     at ebb, alike flow, of a tide,
     all dance,) unite to bepraise
     that crown'd Goddes', ador'd Kŏrê,     1085
      and Maiä the blest saint!

63

SECOND KHOREUTES, *continuing, alluding to* IôN,
> A rogue, who hopes to usurp pow'r,
> and steal the town's hoarded wealth——

FULL KHOROS, *interrupting,*
> an outcast of Apollôn's!

FIRST HEMIKHOROS, *to audience.*   (KHOROS *ceases to dance.*)   *Antistrophè* 2.
> Beware, ye bards, ere ye the Muse seek,                    1090
> when ye sing those malicious, abusive odes, all
> on " lechery womanish, eke profane
> " Cyprian irregular, vapid amours,"
> for ye know that we girls excel, by
> picty, all of ye, bad men!                    1095

SECOND HEMIKHOROS,
> In our chant a retort hear!

FULL KHOROS,
> Go, Muse, sing, sing to the males
> " Curse fall on ye, faithles' husbands"!

FIRST KHOREUTES, *to* KHOROS,
> Ungrateful is he to be dubb'd
> who from Zeus boasts a descent——                    1100

SECOND KHOREUTES, *to* KHOROS,
> *he* waits not to receive, betimes,
> babes born at his home, our
> queen's gifts, but courts Aphrŏdîtê——

FULL KHOROS, *interrupting,*
> elsewhere doth he pay devòirs,
> a son gains from a base source.—                    1105

*End of Prosode—Curtain closes.*

*Interlude the Second.*

KHOROS, *in the orchestra, performs a dance, employing timbrels and wooden and metal cymbals, in addition to its other instruments.*

8

64

### EXODE.

*The curtain opens. Scene as before. Time, approach of dawn.*

*Enter, by left parodos,* THERAPÔN, *in haste, who advances and occupies the logeion.*

*Iambic.*

THERAPÔN, *to* KHOROS *in the orchestra.*

> Say, gentlewomen, where shall I my lady find,
> Erektheus' daughter? Through the city's mazy streets,
> with care extreme, I've search'd, but fail'd to meet the queen.

FIRST KHOREUTES,

> What is 't, my fellow servant? Why in eager haste
> ha'st come? What stirring news ha'st thou to tell thy friends?          1110

THERAPÔN,

> Pursu'd are we. The princely chiefs, who rule the land,
> are tracking her, that caught she be and ston'd to death!

SECOND KHOREUTES,

> Ah me! What say'st? We, surely, not detected are
> in laying secret plots t' assassinate a lad?

THERAPÔN,

> Know, then, ye are, and hence, in worst of plights ye stand!          1115

FIRST KHOREUTES,

> And how was brought to light so well conceal'd a scheme?

THERAPÔN,

> That Justice such unjust designs should thwart, the God
> contriv'd; he chose to keep his purlieus undefil'd.

SECOND KHOREUTES,

> But how? With earnestness I beg thee, tell me, how?

FULL KHOROS,

> E'en now we know that death awaits us: rather we          1120
> would die than live, if slain 's to be our patroness!

THERAPÔN, (KHOROS *accompanying his speech with pantomime,*)

> When Xouthos, queen Kreousa's spouse, had left the shrine
> oracular, with son just gain'd, he, first, bespoke

a feast ; next, cattle bought for sacrifice, for he
was bound, on pilgrimage, to hail the saintly flame          1125
Bakkheíon, and Díonûsos' own-peak'd mount to tinge
with victims' blood, thank-off'ring meet for child acquir'd.—
On setting forth with droves of calves, said he, " my boy,
" stay here ; erected see, by active artisans,
" a large four-corner'd tent ; if, rend'ring vows to Gods,          1130
" who over births preside, detain'd I be, when all 's
" prepar'd, regale thy friends ! "—Iôn the rites prescrib'd
perform'd, then, on the ground, with ropes, a plethron each
in length, trac'd four rectangles ; hence, contain'd the square
of feet a myriad ; (so said they who ought to know ;)          1135
such area needed was, all Delphoi bidden were.—
A spacious booth's surrounding canvass-sheets he lash'd
to standard posts ; next, Hêlios' vivid blaze he screen'd,
in careful guise, that neither noonday rays, nor e'en
declining gleams, should scorch or incommode the guests :          1140
a partial roof he shap'd with awnings haul'd aloft,
which dazzle human eyes ; the temple-veils they were ;
('mongst them, from treasure-chests procur'd, were costly shawls ;
all these as off'rings gat the God from Hêrăklês,
Zeus' son, the spoils he 'd stripp'd from quell'd Amàzŏnes ;)          1145
thereon have skill'd embroid'rers striv'n to represent,
in Aîthêr's vault, the planisphere of Ourănos,—
To goal where sinks his glare impels his fi'ry steeds
refulgent Hêlíos, dragging onwards Hespĕros :
there, Nûx, in sable weeds, her chariot urgeth on ;          1150
(a traceless yoke is her's ;) the Goddess stars attend,
for there the wand'ring Pleias glides through airy space :
there's Orïôn, with brandish'd sword : above, around
the golden pole, by train escorted Arktos wheels :
Sĕlênê, who the months divides, from circle full,          1155
her beams shoots upwards : Hŭădĕs, who with trusty signs

the sailors aid, shine there : Eôs' pale Phôsphŏros
the fleeing orbs pursues.—The hempen sides he hung
with tapestries on rich barbaric tissue wrought ;
there float the well mann'd ships which 'gainst Hellênes warr'd ;    1160
there semibestial folk, there mounted huntsmen are
who run down stags, and savage lions seek to spear;
his female offspring round him, Cekrôps, near the door,
evolves his coils ; (from some Athenian chief a gift
this textile fabric was.)—When glitter'd all the boards    1165
with cups of gold, the sewer the dais ascended ; he
announc'd that those who stood without, might, when they pleas'd,
step in and seated be. So when, in gala garb,
a crowd, with garlands deck'd, had fill'd the close, a choice
repast all spirits cheer'd : when that delight was o'er,    1170
our Presbûs hurri'd in, head steward's part to play,
and laughter 'mongst the jovial crew he rous'd by queer,
abnormal eagerness, for drinking water he
pour'd forth for hands' ablutions, th' incense gum he burnt
to spread perfûme, the sumptuous goblets all he claim'd,    1175
as his especial privilege, alike, to charge.—
So, when approach'd the time the tuneful flutes to breathe,
and crown the common urn, the vet'ran cried, " Away
" with these small vessels, bigger far produce,
" for, well I wot, with joy they sooner warm the heart!"—    1180
The slaves bestirr'd themselves to fetch great chalices
of precious metals ; Presbûs chose the most superb,
and brimful tender'd it his master, (styl'd so now,)
as if to show respect. (He 'midst the potion had
dropp'd drastic poison, which his mistress, it appears,    1185
gave him t' insure the youth's decease, but ignorant
were all of this.) Just as, libations due to make,
our new-found lord, his comrades too, had rais'd the bowls,
from some domestic's lips a bitter curse escap'd ;

the host, by priests instructed, (rear'd within a nave,)                    1190
an evil omen mark'd ; for bev'rage fresh he call'd
in other tankards ; what was meant for Gods upon
the ground he shed, and all enjoin'd to do the same.—
Then, solemn silence reign'd.—With purest lymph, i'mix'd
with Biblis' wine, the votive flagons we supplied :                         1195
amid this service enter'd, flutt'ring through the place,
a flock of doves who roost inside the Loxian walls ;
(a tam'd and petted brood ;) the streaming liquor when
they spied, and plung'd (a raging thirst inclin'd to slake,)
their beaks therein, and gorg'd their feather'd throats therewith,          1200
what brought had been for Deities harmless was to all ;
but, settled one bird where our prince had spill'd the draught,
and, when she tasted that, her wings, her body shook
convuls'd ; in plaintive tones, delirious-wise, she chirp'd
faint falt'ring notes ; (intense surprise pervaded all                      1205
the rev'llers who the creature's agonies beheld ;)
'mid palpitating throes, she droop'd her purple claws
and died.—From off his limbs the heir (by holy spell
declar'd,) detach'd his robe ; then, o'er the table stretch'd,
and shouted " who, 'mongst mortals, *me* to kill designs ?                  1210
" Explain, old wretch, 'twas thou who so officious was't,
" and I 've, e'en now, from thee that baleful stoup receiv'd ! "
He grasp'd our Presbus' arm, in flagrant act that he
might captur'd be, and question'd there, without delay.—
All soon discover'd was ; confess'd he, 'gainst his will,                   1215
and told about Kreousa's plot and deadly brew.
Then, hasten'd out, with all his goodly company,
by voice prophetic honour'd, Loxias' serf elect
who, station'd 'midst the Pûthion magistrates, declaim'd,
" ô gracious Gaiä, hear !   By potent venom would                          1220
" a stranger, King Erektheus' daughter, cause my death " !

.    .    .    .    .    .    .    .

The Delphik judges rul'd, by vote unanimous,
that dash'd from rocks should be our patroness, as one
who 'd hatch'd a murd'rous scheme, within the sanctu'ry,
and tried to slay the Hieros.—Citizens all unite                    1225
to track the woeful dame, on woeful journey sped;
desiring issue, she at Phoibos' fane arrives,
where loseth she all hope of babes, and life as well.—

*Exit* THERAPÔN *by right parodos.*


Ode 8.  MONOSTROPHICA—KHOROS—LYRIC.

FIRST KHOREUTES, *to* KHOROS,                              *Strophè* 1.
    Friends, hope we 've none from Thănătŏs
    of a reprieve!                                            1230
SECOND KHOREUTES,
             What a grief 's mine!
FIRST KHOREUTES,
    Treachery, *our* treachery is all known!
SECOND KHOREUTES,
    Knów that draught which we sent!
FIRST KHOREUTES,
                 Blood of a snake the wine
    to mix with!
SECOND KHOREUTES,
          'Twas a dose compos'd to Death evoke!
FIRST KHOREUTES,
    T' offer a prize to the Gods below!
SECOND KHOREUTES,                                         *Strophè* 2.
    Here be ills thro' my life to mourn!                      1235
FIRST KHOREUTES,
    And by flints to be crush'd our own good queen 's doom'd!
SECOND KHOREUTES,
    Flit i' the air upon wings can *I* ?

FIRST KHOREUTES,

> Or, in a cave, i' the depths of Earth, can *I* death
> from a stone (missile of Âtê,) to escape manage ?

SECOND KHOREUTES,

> A four-hors'd,             1240
> swift car *must* I mount ?

FIRST KHOREUTES

> Or at once
> seek safe berth in a ship's stern ?

FULL KHOROS,          *Epôdê.*

> Ne'er, ne'er can we hide anywhere, should God
> to our aid come not !

FIRST KKOREUTES, *in contemplation,*

> But what woe, my a'griev'd, dear lady, thy heart     1245
> is bound to a'flict !

KORUPHAIOS, *to audience,*

> If we devise means
> wherewith to despite wreak upon others,
> surely, 'tis *our* due to be punish'd !

*Enter* KREOUSA, *in haste and agitation, from left parodos.*

KREOUSA, *to* KHOROS,         *Trochaic.*

> Prospolloi, a crowd pursues me ! Ghastly Slaughter dogs my steps !   1250
> Doom'd by Pûthion vote decisive, public outlaw I 've become !

FIRST KHOREUTES,

> Wretched queen, thy gruesome sentence, all thy peril well we know.

KREOUSA,

> Where to flee ? From Death impending lately narrow 'scape had I,
> and, by stealth the hostel leaving, here I 've rush'd to baulk my foes !

KORUPHAIOS,

> Where, oh where but Phoibos' altar ?          1255

KREOUSA, *to* KORUPHAIOS,

> What can that avail me now ?

KORUPHAIOS,
Suppliant there to kill 's illegal.

KREOUSA,
Yet the Law would take my life!

KORUPHAIOS,
Should the hand of Man arrest thee.

KREOUSA,
Even now the angry guards
hither swarm, with threat'ning weapons!

KORUPHAIOS,
Mount the steps, assume thy seat!
Should'st be slain, though temple-shelter'd, well assur'd be thou thy blood
would return on those who spill'd it! Bow to what Tükhê decrees! 1260

KREOUSA *sits on the upper step of the altar, upon which she lays her hand. Shouts, howls and groans are heard from without. Enter* IÔN, *in gala tunic, crowned with roses, unarmed, and without chlamys, bow or quiver, followed by the Delphik town guards bearing torches. All rush in hastily, but, seeing* KREOUSA *at the altar, cease to advance.*

IÔN, *in contemplation,*                                    *Iambic.*
O Tauromorphous-visag'd father Cêphïsos,
what viper ha'st engender'd, whose despiteful eyes
with rage intensely glare, and glow with bloody flame,
whose nature matcheth well, in Mischief's deadly bent,
the Gorgôn's venom-drops she sought to slay me with?      1265

(*To the Guards*)
Seize, drag her forth, and let those dainty curls of hair
be torn sheer off by bleak Parnêsos' flinty scarrs,
from whose projecting crags compell'd be she to leap!

(*The soldiers whisper to one another, and seem to hesitate.* IÔN *continues, in contemplation,*)
A lucky chance I 've met with, ere I reach'd the town
of Pallas, 'neath my stepdame's influence to fall,       1270

for, safe amidst my friends, I've gaug'd her temper well,
of me her hate malignant clearly I 've descried!

(*To* KREOUSA, *advancing towards her*)

    Had I been closely trapp'd within thy palace walls,
    thou would'st to Haides' house have soon dispatch'd me straight!
    But neither Lord Apollôn's pyre, nor holy fane,       1275
    shall save thy life!  To thee no pity 's due——

(*Aside, and sobbing hysterically*)        reserv'd

    be all for me, my mother too, in person, who,
    though ever absent, always occupies my thoughts!—

(*To the guards*)

    Behold that cunning wretch!  What crafty webs on webs
    she works!  The God's high altar now she croucheth at,      1280
    due punishment for crime she hopes, thereby, to shun!

KREOUSA, *rising, in defiant attitude,*

    On mine account, and that of this great God, before
    whose shrine I stand, take heed!  I warn thee, slay me not!

IÔN,

    In common what can be 'tween thee and Loxias?

KREOUSA,

    That sacred is to him my person I profess!       1285

IÔN,

    Yet me thou'dst kill with poison, "sacred" though to him.

KREOUSA,

    No longer "Phoibos' boy," thy father's ar't thou now!

IÔN,

    That God's I was, I tell thee, ere my sire appear'd.

KREOUSA,

    But "sacred" ar't thou not, nor was't, as I'm to him.

IÔN,

    Thou ar't not pious, though, and pious aye was I.       1290

KREOUSA,

    My race's foe I deem'd thee, hence I sought thy life.

IÔN, *indicating that he is unarmed,*

> But not with sword meant I to march towards thy realm.

KREOUSA,

> With worst intent, thou meant'st Erektheus' house to fire!

IÔN,

> Where lie the quick'ning brands?   Where glows the steady flame?

KREOUSA,

> To dwell with me and seize my wealth was thy design.                1295

IÔN,

> My sire may choose to give me land which he 's acquired.

KREOUSA,

> In Pallas' "land" what voice hath son of Aiŏlos?

IÔN,

> He needeth none; his spear, not "voice," that "land" preserv'd.

KREOUSA,

> But ne'er may be a hir'd ally of "land" possess'd.

IÔN,

> What prompted thee to slay me?   Had'st thou ought to dread?        1300

KREOUSA,

> If spar'd I thy young life, I fear'd to lose my own.

IÔN, *pointedly,*

> Did'st envy, childless wife, my sire who found me here?

KREOUSA, *scornfully,*

> Would'st seek to sack a home devoid of sons' defence?

IÔN,

> Should I receive no share of what my father owns?

KREOUSA, *as before,*

> What gain'd his shield—and "spear," for that 's thy heritage.       1305

IÔN, *angrily,*

> This altar quit, divine afflatus' holy seat!

KREOUSA, *as before,*

> Thy mother rail at, more than me, where'er she be!

Iôn,

> Would'st hope to murder plot, and penalties escape?

Kreousa,

> Oh, no! Within the cella slay me, an thou wi'lt!

Iôn,

> Amid the God's green wreaths why would'st prefer to die? 1310

Kreousa,

> 'Twould sorrow cause to one who sorrow caus'd to me.
> Phew! (*sobbing hysterically, she sinks upon the altar-steps.*)

Koruphaios, *to audience,*

> How wond'rous 'tis that Gods for mortals should a Law
> ordain, which seems unfair, of reason quite devoid!
> On hallow'd altars persons vile should ne'er recline,
> but chas'd should be therefrom; what appertains to Gods 1315
> no wicked hands should touch. Let only worthy folk,
> who 've grossly injur'd been, asylum there assume!
> That good and bad, alike, should reach the same resort,
> and gain from Gods the same defence, unjust appears!

Iôn, *perceiving the guards disinclined to obey his orders, advances to drag* Kreousa *from the altar, when enter* Puthia *from the central door of the temple. She carries a child's cradle, festooned with garlands of coloured wool. The guards make humble reverence to her, and fall back. She places her burthen upon the peristyle steps.*

Puthia, *to* Iôn,

> Stay, son, for I, amongst the Delphik sisterhood, 1320
> by ancient law elect, Apollôn's prophetess,
> my wonted seat, the sacred trĭpŏd, have left in haste,
> and o'er the cella's threshold stepp'd to come to thee!

Iôn, *to* Puthia, *embracing her,*

> All hail, dear mother, though I owe thee not my birth!

Puthia,

> Thou 'st always call'd me so, and sweet 's the name to me. 1325

Iôn, *indicating* Kreousa,

    Ha'st heard that *she* with subtle plots would take my life?

Puthia,

    I've heard so.—Thou by impulse rash misguided art.

Iôn,

    What?  Those who seek to slay me ought I not to slay?

Puthia,

    'Gainst step-sons, wives are ever wont to bear a grudge.

Iôn,

    Ay, treatment infamous my step-dame's shown to me.

Puthia,

    Regard it not!  This temple quit, and reach thy home!

Iôn,

    Accepting thine advice, what course adopt should I?

Puthia,

    With omens fair, Athênai enter, free from wrong!

Iôn,

    Certes, he 's " freed from wrong " who 's kill'd a deadly foe.

Puthia,

    But kill not her!  To what my speech imports attend!

Iôn,

    Speak on!  Well meant thou ar't, I know, whate'er thou say'st.

Puthia, *indicating the cradle,*

    Did'st note that basket borne, just now, between my arms?

Iôn,

    With garlands deck'd an antique hamper I descry.

Puthia,

    In *that* I rais'd thee, once, a baby newly born.

Iôn,

    What say'st?  A story surgeth up ne'er heard before.

Puthia,

    I 've always held it secret ; now shall all be told.

Iôn,

    But what thou had'st of mine why ha'st conceal'd so long?

Puthia,

    To keep thee 'neath his roof, as serf, the God desir'd.

Ión,

    He wants me now no more ?   What proof of that have I ?

Puthia,

    To other clime he sends thee, stating who 's thy sire.        1345

Ión,

    And why that bassinet ha'st retained ?   By order was 't ?

Puthia,

    By inspiration 'twas, direct, from Loxĩas.

Ión,

    To serve what purpose say !   With thy discourse proceed !

Puthia,

    Until the present time the treasure-trove to guard.

Ión,

    And what wil 't now disclose ?   Wil 't bring me gain or harm ?    1350

Puthia,

    Know, boy, the cloth which swath'd thee, first, that cradle holds.

Ión,

    Wherewith to seek my mother ha'st thou brought me clues ?

Puthia,

    E'en so, by this God's wish, though ne'er till now express'd.

Ión,

    Bright gleams of future bliss this happy day presents !

Puthia,

    This object take, and her who bore thee strive to find !       1355

Ión,

    To Europe's bounds and Asia's, too, is 't mine to go ?

Puthia,

    How far thou 'lt have to learn.   To please the God, my child,
    with care I 've nurtur'd thee ; these relics, now, to thee
    I give, which HE, although he never *bade* me, *wish'd*
    me safe to keep, though, why he did so wot not I.—       1360

That I 've these weeds possess'd no mortal creature e'er
hath known, or seen the place wherein they hidden were.—
Farewell!  As wer't my son, this fond embrace receive!—

*(Here she embraces* IÔN.*)*

Thy mother straight to search for prudent schemes devise!
So, first, investigate if Delphik damosel                          1365
produc'd and laid thee down before this temple-gate,
and next, if girl Hellênik plac'd thee there!  Thou ha'st
my blessing, that of Phoibos too who guards thy state.—

IÔN *kneels, and* PUTHIA, *having placed her hands upon his head, re-enters the temple.*

IÔN *(rising and sobbing hysterically), in contemplation,*

Phew!  Phew!  It wrings my heart, with tears it floods my eyes
to think that she who bore me, fruit of chance amour           1370
which clos'd a night's debauch, her breast denied me, sold,
or pack'd me off in secret ; hence, a nameless waif,
a servile life I've led within this God's demesne!

*(Here he starts, and makes reverence to* PHOIBOS' *statue.)*

(All good my God hath sent me ; that which evil is
my Dâimôn.)   During time in which I might caress'd          1375
have been, between my mother's arms, and pass'd thro' years
of bliss, of all her fost'ring care I 've been depriv'd.
But she, who brought me forth, must wretched be ; she hath
despoil'd herself of every joy a son supplies.—

*(Here he lifts the cradle from the peristyle steps.)*

With this unopen'd basket I'll present the Lord,                  1380
lest it discover proofs of what I'm loth to know.
If she, who gave me birth, hath chanc'd a slave to be,
far worse it were to find than deem her lost to me.—

*(Here he kneels before* PHOIBOS' *statue.)*

O Phoibos, in thy nave a vot'ry's gift accept!

*(Advancing towards the temple, he starts, suddenly, and returns.)*

What act is mine?   Ought I to thus misprize my God's     1385
benevolence, which sav'd me means wherewith to find
my mother?   No, I 'll dare the panier's lid to raise,
for none need think to shun their Destinies' decrees.

*(Here he unfastens the buckles of the cradle.)*

O sacred wreaths and bandages, why have ye kept
so long conceal'd what most important is to me?     1390
See how the rocking-cradle's wicker envelope
remains quite fresh, by influence divine preserv'd;
its osier-plaits no mildew show, although've elaps'd
long years since charg'd it was with wares, whate'er they be!

KREOUSA, *who has watched* IÔN'S *actions with intense interest, clasps her hands, and utters a cry.*

KREOUSA,
Blest vision!   What unlook'd for object meets my gaze?     1395
IÔN, *to* KREOUSA,
Hush!   Well thou know'st of pungent words thou'st said enough.
KREOUSA,
Of silence tell me not!   From speech I can't refrain.
The ark I see wherein I laid thee, long ago,
(when thou a new-born baby was't, my only son,)
in king Cĕkrôps' dark cavern 'mongst the rocks Măkrai!     1400
Desert this pyre must I, though instant death be mine!

*She descends the altar steps and runs towards the cradle.*

IÔN, *to the guards, two of whom arrest* KREOUSA,
Seize, seize her straight!   By some great God she stricken is
with madness.   See, she leaves the altar!   Bind her arms!

KREOUSA *breaks away from the guards, and, with one hand grasps the skirts of* IÔN'S *tunic, and with the other the cradle.*

KREOUSA, *to* IÔN,
>My slaughter spare ye not, but let me cling to thee,
>and this, and what belongs to thee enclos'd therein!　　　　1405

IÔN, *to the guards, who re-arrest and withdraw her, somewhat,*
>Here 's impudence!　She 'd kidnap me on false pretence.

KREOUSA,
>Oh no!　Thou 'rt found by one who loves thee!　Dear thou ar't ——

IÔN,
>If dear am I to thee, why seek to plot my death?

KREOUSA, *continuing,*
>for dear to her who bore him ought a son to be.

IÔN,
>Cease wily nets to weave!　*Thee*, soon, I'll nicely catch!　　　　1410

KREOUSA (*aside*),
>Oh how I wish thou may'st!　I aim at that, my child!

IÔN,
>This basket, empty is it?　(KREOUSA *makes a sign in the negative.*)
>　　　　　Fill'd is it with what?

KREOUSA,
>The clothes which thou was't swath'd in, when laid out by me.

IÔN,
>And, ere thou seest them, can'st those garments specify?

KREOUSA,
>That I correctly state them gage would I my life!　　　　1415

IÔN,
>Say, what be they?　(*Aside*) How marv'llous seems thy confidence!

KREOUSA,
>First, find a woven shawl, in childhood wrought by me!

IÔN,
>How made?　In textile skill young wenches vary much.

KREOUSA,
>Rude, incomplete, my shuttle's sampler only 'twas.

IôN,

    What figure's broider'd on 't?   (*Aside.*) Thou can'st not trick me now! **1420**

KREOUSA,

    The peplos' middle threads a Gorgôn bear, display'd—

IôN (*aside*),

    O mighty Zeus, what Fate unerring hunts me down?

KREOUSA, *continuing*,

    by circling coils of serpents border'd, Aigis-wise.

IôN, *exhibiting the peplos*,

    Behold!

(*aside*) Describ'd as though by God's spell, here 's disclos'd the web!

KREOUSA,

    My girlish treadle's early work! I mind it well.           **1425**

IôN.

    What else is here?   Can'st make, of lucky hits, but one?

KREOUSA,

    Two golden snakes whose jaws with grins malicious yawn.

IôN,

    For what especial purpose are such gauds design'd?

KREOUSA,

    Round necks of certain infants clasp'd to be, my son.

    Mementos ancient they!  To King Erĭkthŏnios          **1430**

    said Pallas, "let thy race wear trinkets like my gifts!"

IôN,

    Ay, here they are.   What third deposit yet remains?

KREOUSA,

    Around thy baby-brow I wound an olive wreath,

    from plants which, erst, Athênê 'mongst my cliffs produc'd;

    if such be there, its verdure fresh it still retains,         **1435**

    because 'twas cut from shrubs which suffer no decay.

*At a sign from* IôN, *the guards release* KREOUSA, *and fall back.* IôN *advances to*
    KREOUSA *and embraces her.*

IÔN,

    Thee, dearest mother mine, with transport I behold!
    At last, with heart-felt joy, I kiss thy gentle face!

KREOUSA,

    O boy, thy mother's light, transcending Helios' own,
        (*here she makes reverence to Phoibos' statue*)
    (excuse such words, ô God!) I clip thee 'tween my arms,    1440
    whom ne'er again I thought to view!  Beneath the earth,
    I fear'd thou might'st be hous'd with Persĕphŏnê, the queen!

IÔN,

    My cherish'd parent, then must I, embrac'd by thee,
    resemble one who died, and rose to life again!

    *Ode 9.  Duo.  Monostrophica.*            *Lyric.*

KREOUSA, *gazing on the sky,*           *Strophè.*

      Iô! Iô! Aithêr's luminous wide domain,    1445
    with what shout 's thy blue vault to be pierc'd?  For whence comes
        tŏ mĕ joy unexpected, whence a'rives tŏ mĕ
            such una'loy'd delight?

IÔN,

    Of all events which deem 'd I, Maiă, possible,
    what least my mind struck was to find that I 'm thy son.    1450

KREOUSA, *glancing at the guards,*        *Strophè 2.*

           Yet in alarm am I!

IÔN, *tenderly,*

           Know'st not that I 'm beside thee?

KREOUSA,

           Hope of happines'
           all to be lost a'pear'd!

        (*apostrophizing* PUTHIA)
    Iô! Oh where, from whom, madam, why, did ye receive
        set in your arms my babe?
    Prithe', who took him away to domes Loxïan?    1455

IÔN (*with reverential gesture*),                                              *Iambic.*

     Just so God's will was done !—Our portion is to joy
     as much in present bliss as mourn'd we have in woe.

KREOUSA,                              *Lyric.*   *Strophè*, 3.

     Much shĕ dĭd weep whenas thy birth happ'd, my child,
     but wail'd thy mother, when she *thee* abandon'd !
     Now, to caress thy cheeks giveth a life renew'd ;          1460
     verily, cheers mĕ bliss my tongue fails t' express !

IÔN,                                           *Iambic.*

     Those last fond words of thine I 'd fain have said to thee.

KREOUSA, *exultingly*,                       *Lyric.*   *Strophè*, 4.

       No more am I a childles' wretch, of hope 'reft !
       Firm sits my grand race ; gains the land Turannoi ;
              afresh blooms Erèktheus !          1465
    So, ye children of Earth, shal'ye peer thro' a murky night no more ;
     soon shal' ye all behold a light—Hêlios' own !——

*She pauses and seems absorbed in contemplation.* IÔN *steals towards her, and passes his arm round her waist.*

IÔN, *tenderly*,                                    *Iambic.*

     Maiê belov'd, when comes my sire to take me hence,
     of joy I've brought to thee may *he* receive a share ?

KREOUSA, *hiding her mask*,                   *Lyric. Strophè* 5.

     O my son, my son, what ask'st ?  Ah, whàt, ah what—what a charge
          to meet ?          1470

IÔN,

     What say'st, dear ?

KREOUSA,

          *He* thy sire ?  Oh no, it was—other who—

IÔN, *wailing*,

     Aï !  Did'st, when young, a birth debas'd a'sign tŏ mĕ ?

KREOUSA, *sadly*,

            Not by a torch alight,
            not with a dance by night,

hўmĕmæl had I, 1475
ere as a son thou cam'st tŏ mĕ!

IÔN, *Strophè 6.*

Ai! Born was I a spurious waif? Whom from, mother?

KREOUSA, *extending her arms towards the pediment,*

Well know Gorgŏphŏnè——

IÔN,

Why speak'st such wild words?

KREOUSA, *continuing,*

(who, by my crags, has a seat
on a hill which a'fords verdant oil-plants)— 1480

IÔN,

Thou tell'st, thou tell'st some parable; dark's the sense ŏf ĭt!

KREOUSA, *continuing,*

on a rock by the birds a'tun'd, Phoibos——

IÔN, *Strophè 7.*

My Phoibos? What say'st?

KREOUSA, *continuing,*

lay bў mĕ once; 'twas a fact none knew.—

IÔN, *aside, ironically,* *Iambic.*

Speak on, for *me* thou tell'st of chance most fortunate!

KREOUSA, *Lyric.* 1485

Then a babe by the God had I (thy birth's
secret was well kept), when a tenth moon shone.

IÔN, *aside,*

Brave were thy news, dame, could thy tale be credible!

KREOUSA, *Strophè 8.*

Girl's peplos in a loom wrought had I;
(copy rude wăs ĭt of one which had wov'n 1490
my mother) it was wrapp'd round thee:
the milk by breast maternal was, my dear son,
denied to thee; not e'en to bathe thee stay'd I,
for at once, in a cave, to fierce vultures
feast, seiz'd, rent to be by claws, cast thou wast, 1495
Haidês' sweet, young prize!

IÔN, *shuddering*,                                                    *Strophè* 9.
      How cruel was't thou, mother!
KREOUSA,
      Alarm'd, mad, in a panic, I thy life risk'd,
          tho' to destroy thee, my
          child, I 'd not a wish.                    1500
*Here* IÔN *dismisses the guards, who retire by left parŏdos.*

IÔN, *coldly, to* KREOUSA,
      Law allows not *me* to thy Death sanction.
KREOUSA,                                                               *Epôdê.*
      Iô, Iô!  Dire lot thro' life ever had I;
   dire can it yet be, for hastily emerge we,
      toss'd from a sea of A'fliction,                      1505
      Happines' heights to ascend.—
      Thou, shifted wind, com'st balmily;
      stop awhile, for enough have we had of a storm!—
      Arisen has a wind, no more an ill one, child!

KORUPHAIOS, *to audience*,                                            *Iambic.*
      Regarding such events as these, 'tis well to say,     1510
      " no mortal e'er should deem a state devoid of hope."

IÔN, *in contemplation*,
      O thou, who bring'st to human race's myriads
      a change from Mis'ry sad to blithe Felicity,
      Tŭkhê, why came to me that stage in life, when I
      my mother might have slain, an impious act achiev'd?   1515
      Phew! (*sighing.*)

KORUPHAIOS *to audience*,
      A bootless query's that!  'Neath Helios' beams occur,
      each day, events whose cause we vainly seek to know.—
IÔN, *to* KREOUSA,
      I 've found in thee, my mother, all I most esteem;
      mescems at kin of thine can none be found to fleer;

yet, somewhat I to tell thee wish, and thee alone.— 1520
Draw near! Within thine ear I fain would whisper words,
and o'er thine early errors closely draw a veil.—
If thou has't stepp'd awry, my mother, whilst a girl,
take heed ere chargest thou a God with all the blame
for lapse of thine, by cause of frailty feminine, 1525
and, bent on hiding our disgrace, aware a babe,
by Gods, could n'er be thine, say'st Pûthios' son am I!

KREOUSA, *extending her arms towards the pediment,*

I swear by great Athênê-Nîcê, who to Zeus,
'gainst Gaiä's sons, with spear, in chariot, brought her aid,
no mortal man thy genuine parent was, my boy; 1530
thy sire is he who rear'd thee, Loxïas, the prince.

IÔN,

Why sought he other father, then, for child of his?
Why said he, 'midst his fane, that Xouthos' own was I?

KREOUSA,

He said not Xouthos got thee; gave he thee to him,
no less his Self thy sire. Hath not a friend the right 1535
to yield his son to friend, his household train to guide?

IÔN,

A doubt if this God's spell be true, or grossly false,
as well it may, my mother, much disturbs my mind.

KREOUSA,

Now, hear, my dear, how seems to me the case to stand!—
For thine advantage placeth thee in royal halls 1540
Lord Loxïas; should'st thou that God's own son be styl'd,
thou ne'er could'st hold my race's rich inheritance,
nor bear a Father's name. Whose could'st thou? Secret I
my union kept, and thee I hid, and left to die.—
For thee, to do thee boot, a titular sire he finds.— 1545

IÔN,

By shallow phantasies like these I 'll not be led,

but, hast'ning through this nave, I 'll straightway Phoibos ask
if I 'm from human creature sprung; if Loxïas'——

*Reiterated peals of thunder are heard, and broad sheets of flame flash, in rapid*
*   succession, over the altar.   A machine descends from the scenic clouds; it*
*   represents a chariot preceded by four unyoked horses, whose heads are towards the*
*   spectators; in the car stands Pallas, furnished with spear, shield and helmet; the*
*   machine remains suspended till the close of the drama; the Goddess and her*
*   vehicle are supposed to be seen, only, by the spectators in the auditorium.*

Iôn, *continuing,*

   Eah! What Deity, hov'ring o'er this holy shrine,
   a spectacle displays which dazzles like the Sun?                    1550
   Let 's flee, my mother, lest Gods present we behold
   before our time arrive their glorious forms to view!

Iôn *and* Kreousa, *with joined hands, in the act of escaping, on hearing the voice of*
   Pallas, *fall on their knees.*

Pallas, *to* Iôn *and* Kreousa,

   Flee not!   Nay, shun not ME (as if I meant ye harm),
   in fair Athênai's clime propitious, here as well!—
   I come from that grac'd town of yours which bears my name,           1555
   I, Pallas, hither sent on Loxïas' behest,
   [who deems it indiscreet amongst ye here to be,
   lest shent he chance to find himself for certain acts!]

*to* Iôn,

   He biddeth me t' accost thee, youth, and tell to thee
   that he by yonder woman really is thy sire;                          1560
   if gives he thee to one who got thee not, it is
   that he thy state secure may make in royal halls:
   and, when to all his spell became interpreted,
   he, fearing lest thy mother's schemes should cause thy death,
   and thence her own, by means extrinsic sav'd ye both.—              1565
   That Lord hath will'd that all these facts be secret held

in Pallas' realm, that only thou and this thy queen
should know that thou to her and Phoibos ow'st thy birth.—

*to* KREOUSA,

    Accomplish'd be my mission!  Hear the strict commands
of that great God, at whose request I 've yok'd my car!      1570
Kreousa, lead to Cekrŏps' stately burgh thy boy,
on thine imperial throne enable him to sit ;
Erektheus claim can he as his progenitor,
hence, o'er my land to reign, in justice, hath the right !—
Through each Hellênik province fame shall he acquire:      1575
from him, from root unique, shall spring four mighty sons,
who 'll lend their names to sep'rate tribes distributed
amongst the regions which surround my rocky mount :
Gĕlĕôn the first ; the next Hoplêtes shall be styl'd ;
next Argădeis ; the last shall rule a single race,      1580
mine Aigis-mail to honour, Aigikŏreis yclep'd :
in time shall those brave chiefs succeeded be by sons,
who 'll dwell in cities built on isles of Kûklădes,
and continental shores ; hence, strengthen my domain.
The mainlands both, on either side, they 'll colonize,      1585
the wealthy Asian countries hold in permanence,
And Eurôpaion, too ; on young Iôn's account,
Iônes titled, they shall signal glory gain.—
Know thou and Xouthos, soon, shall be with issue blest:
Dôros, from whom the Dôris clan shall rise, renown'd ;      1590
Akhaios next, on Pĕlŏpian soil who domicil'd,
of sea-coasts near Rhĭôn the prince shall be proclaim'd,
and all the people, who those districts wide frequent,
will boast of nomenclature famous made by him.—
All well hath Phoibos done ; its illness subsequent      1595
he spar'd thy travail, hence unknown to all thy friends.
When thou thine infant had'st produc'd, and hidden him,
array'd in swaddling clothes, he sent Hermês to raise

and, carried 'twixt his arms, to expedite him here,
where nurs'd he well the babe, whose life he thus preserv'd.—            1600
The status keep conceal'd of him who gat thy child,
by sweet conceit possess'd that Xouthos happy rest,
and thou, in peace, my dame, thy blessings duly prize !—
Rejoice ! Of cheery lot I bring ye both the news ;
a welcome breathing-space and truce from ills are yours !—            1605

IÔN                                                                 *Trochaic.*

Pallas, sov'reign Zeus' wise daughter, trusting thee, receiv'd have I
thine august annunciation, and believe myself to be
Loxias' son, and this dear lady's, mother whom I 've lately deem'd.

KREOUSA, *to* KHOROS,

Hear my voice in praise of Phoibos, worshipp'd not for long by me ;
for the child, I thought neglected, nurtur'd well restoreth he !—            1610
Now, with joy, the God's prophetic seat and portals I behold,
which, till now, appear'd repulsive !

*She passes beneath the portico of the temple, and divesting herself of her crown,*
*bracelets, &c., appends them to the bosses of the doors and lintels.*

See how gladly hang my hands
round the " roptra " all my jewels, how I kneel before the gates !—

*She prostrates herself upon the peristyle's steps, and seems as if in silent prayer.*
*A pause.*

PALLAS, *to* KREOUSA,

I commend thee, brought to reason, eulogizing thus the God.—
Will divine, though tardy seeming, ne'er omits its pow'r to show.—            1615

*After a flourish of trumpets within, is enacted a dumb show. Advances, from the temple,*
*a procession of priests and therapes, preceded by the five hosioi and* PUTHIA,
*attended by pages. A herald summons* IÔN, *who kneels and receives the symbol of*
*dispensation, the accolade, and benediction. After another flourish of trumpets,*
*the procession re-enters the temple.—*IÔN *returns to* KREOUSA *and embraces her.*

KREOUSA, *to* IôN,

    Come, my son, let 's hasten homewards !

PALLAS,

                      Lead the way !   I 'll follow thee.

IôN, *to* KREOUSA,

    Best of guards our journey shareth !

KREOUSA,

                      One who loves our city, too.

PALLAS,

    Go, remount thy throne ancestral !

KREOUSA, *embracing* IôN,

                      Worth possessing, now, by me.

*Enter, from the orchestra, the* KHOROS, *followed by the queen's guards, by left parodos. All form into lines and kneel before the altar of* PHOIBOS.

KREOUSA, IôN, *and full* KHOROS,

    Mighty Zeus and Lêtô's offspring, Lord Apollôn, hail to thee !

*A procession is arranged and set in motion ; the car of Pallas hovers over it, and, as* KREOUSA'S *trumpeters sound a flourish, the curtain closes.*

### Epilogue.

KORUPHAIOS *mounts the thymelè, and addresses the audience.*

    Ye, whose hopes mischance hath blighted, firm in faith the Gods adore !
    They, whose lives are pure and blameless, rest, at last, in joy serene,
    while the wicked, unrepenting, ne'er attain t' a blissful end.—

*Here concludes the drama.*

# NOTES.

" The past was made of the same stuff as the present : surely there is no other key that can unlock its true meaning but a profound insight into the present, wherein all is summed up.   How piece together, into coherent types of the whole, the waifs and strays that have floated down on the ocean of time, but by mastering the types and penetrating the meanings as now clothed in living flesh and blood around us ?"—*Anne Gilchrist*.

Smollett, in his tour on the Continent, observes that it is remarkable how slightly customs and superstitions have varied there, since periods of remote antiquity.

93

*The numerals preceding, and cited in, the notes, refer to the lines of the text of this play.*

1 Atlas, a Titan, formerly king of Mauritania, had his task assigned to him as a punishment for his rebellion.
2 The ancient Deities were located in the heavens, the modern at Mount Olympus.
Pleiônê, daughter of Oceanus, was the wife of Atlas.—(*Ov. Fast.* 81, *Apollod.* 1, 3, 10.)
5 Two birds, eagles, doves, or swans, sent from opposite quarters by Zeus, found the centre of Earth by resting at one spot. There the Delphik temple was built. According to the Talmud, the earth's centre was in the valley of Jehoshaphat; according to the Mahomedans, in the mosque of Aksoor, in Jerusalem; and according to the Christians, in the holy sepulchre there.
7 Zeus communicated, exclusively, to Apollo the prescience which he received from Anangkê.
9 A colossal statue of the patroness of Athens stood in its market-place—*Her. Fur.* 1003.
10 See Genesis v. "And the sons of God, &c."
12 The "long rocks" at the entrance of Athens, and, in later times, the walls extending to the Piræus, were called "Makrai."
15 957.
16 To save Kreousa's honour and that of her family:
"nam Deum
"non par videtur facere delictum suum,
"suamque culpam, expetere in mortalem ut siet". *Amph. Plaut.*
17 Pausanias is in error saying that it occurred "in the God's own temple." See 31, 494, 1400.
18 Why she was able to remove the babe, immediately after her *accouchement*, see 1500. She swathed it in the cave, 955.

20 The ancient Hellenes claimed descent from Titans, sons of Gaia (the earth) ;
when Cecrops introduced the cult of the Olympian Gods, and Gaia was no longer
worshipped, the new divinity, Hephaistos, miraculously created, from the earth,
Ericthonios, "verily of the ground."—*Stobæus. Genes.* 2, 7 ; "Adam, red or brown
clay." *Kitto. Ov. Met.* 2, 8. *Lact. F. R.* 162.
Similar traditions are common amongst Orientals.

22 The "virgin" was Pallas. Serpents, when harmless, were considered as tutelary
genii in a dwelling. See, in *Gell's Pompeii*, a print from the fresco of the
" Genius loci." The emperor Tiberius carried one in his *sinus*. *Il corricolo,
Dumas.*

23 Agraulis' daughters were Agraulos, Hersè and Pandrŏsos. *Ov. Met.* 2,553.
Agraulis was wife of Cecrops.

27 1499.

29 Athens is expressed in the plural number to signify its upper and lower towns.

30 The Titans and their mortal descendants ; see note 20.

36 Loxias means "oblique." This name was supposed to refer to the ambiguity
of his oracles, but Macrobius, Sat. 1, 17 (400 A.D.) derives the word from the
refraction of the rays of the sun in atmospheric and aqueous media, which
phænomenon does not appear to have attracted attention in England until the
commencement of the last century, when it was lectured upon at the R. S.
See *Dr. Derham's* letter, with diagram, to D. B. Lennard, *Philos. Trans.* But
Newton, in his Principia, says that it was discovered by Grimaldi, 1660 A.D.

41 Hêlios, the sun, a name of Apollo as its deity. " Hêloyo " was the name of a
Phenician God. Loxias, Puthios, Phoibos, were names of Apollo.

44 The prophetess arrived from the college of priestesses, of which she was principal. Their duties were confined to dancing at sacrifices and in processions ;
to attending to the altar fires and censers; and to blessing and cursing.
*Potter.*

45 To place a new-born infant in the temple courts was sacrilege. *Æschyl.
Chor.* 914.

48 The God inspired her with a disinclination to cast away the child. 1357.

49 Whoever raised an orphan, or foundling infant, from the ground, was
chargeable for its keep, and stood to it in "loco parentis." *Potter.* Thus the

prophetess became a titular mother, though she dedicated the child to Phoibos.  644. 1324. 321.

52 " The choice morsels of the sacrifice were reserved for the use of the priests." *Athen. Deip.* 4. 28.  This apparently trivial circumstance is mentioned to signify that the child was a favourite in the temple, hence to account for his subsequent elevation.

54 The " Delphik chiefs " were styled the five " hosici."  Each of those priests bore the title of " his holiness."  *Potter.*  The bishops of Nicœa were thus denominated, as are now the Pope of Rome and the Greek Patriarch.

55 This boy, æt. 16, holds offices assigned, separately, to distinguished ecclesiastics of the ancient and modern Greek and Roman Churches; he has access to all parts of the temple, except the crypt, (for he is not a priest, though eligible as one,) has undisputed authority in the fane, even to power over life and death, and impunity from committing sacrilege therein.  He cuts the consecrated laurel, which none but the priests may touch.  354. 315. 225. 414. 152. 94. 325. 1502. 1275. 112. 522.  Moreover, he has been devoted to the God, and is styled " Loxias' boy," and the " Hieros."  643. 311. 1225. 1343. 1287. 1218. 821.  He can be readily identified with the Daphnephoros, of which official, Pausanias and Plutarch furnish long accounts.  This functionary, selected by reason of personal and mental excellence, during his boyhood, gathered the laurel in the vale of Tempe, accompanied by a solemn procession, and cut it, when consecrated, for the use of the temple at Delphi.  A branch of this (to touch which was sacrilege,) he carried, amidst Apollo's processions on festal days, " attired in a long robe, with flowing hair."  Such was the costume in which Apollôn-Mousagêtes was represented in his statues. *Propertius. Dodwell. Goëthe.*  " Though not a priest, he performed many sacerdotal duties, had supreme authority in the fane, as 'tamias,' and his person was held so sacrosanct that, to insult him was punishable by death."  It would seem that he was deemed a temporary representative, if not incarnation, of the Apollino, for he is styled, by the above historians, as one " devoted" to that God, and as the " Hieros," precisely as he is in this play. 821. 1225.  Beare (in his *Hermath.* A.D. 1887) says, " Hieros is a word which involves direct relation to a divine person, and, to a Greek, it would have been an unintelligible and profane expression, if applied to a human being."                    12

56 See 315 and note.

59 Xouthos, banished by his brothers, had become a soldier of fortune. *Smith, C.D.*

60 From lines, 290. 298. 721. 724. 813. 1298. 1299, we may conclude that the Eubœans invaded Attica and beleaguered Athens ; that Erectheus summoned Xouthos to his assistance who, with his free-lances, raised the siege and, pursuing the troops of Chalcis across the straits, ravaged their island. *Strabo* 10, 446, says that the "Athenians founded Chalcis before the Trojan war." As a possible "casus belli," Bury adduces a passage from *Apoll. Rhod. and Schol.* 1. 95. "Alkon, with his daughter Khalliope, fled to Euboia ; Erektheus, whom he had offended, demanded his surrender from the Khalkodontides who refused it."

64 No writer but Euripides mentions Aiolos as a son of Zeus.

65 We are here reminded that English, as well as other Europeans, make pilgrimages to the shrine of our Lady at Lourdes, in the Pyrenees, and some of them with the same object as did Xouthos and Kreousa to the shrine of Apollo, at Delphi. In August, 1886 A.D., "ten thousand votaries visited Lourdes." *Standard.* See, in *Croker's Ireland*, an account of the pilgrimage to Gougaun Barra, and of the pattern (patron) fairs.

67 The god could not control the decrees of Anangkê.

68 Apollo had knowledge, only, of mortals' affairs ; of the thoughts and deeds of celestials Zeus alone had cognizance. *Apul. Met.* 8. 57. Hermês, out of curiosity, had visited the crypt, invisibly, and had overheard the priests discussing the terms of the forthcoming oracle. See 77.

72 "Agnized," adopted as heir by Kreousa, ignorant that she was the boy's mother.

75 " Iôn," coming, *eimi*, to " come and to go ; " *erkhomai*, to " come and to go." " The Messiah is " he that cometh, " *ho elthôn*," *John*. 6. 14. Going and Coming, Cumming, Comyn, are common English surnames. Some commentators have traced " Iôn " to Javan, Janus ; others have imagined that it signified the " far east," a " pansy," and " le desiré." In a note, in *Burmann's Ovid. Met.* 13. 4, Muncker quotes Conon on the etymology of the name " Anios." " Anios, son of Apollo and Creusa, was, when an infant, taken by his father to Delphi ; educated there, he became king-priest, ' rex antistes,'

and hospitably received Anchises and Eneas." May not an anagram be suspected here, Anios, Ioans, Iônes, hence Iôn and Johannes?

76 See 224 and note.

77 As Hermes is not to reappear, this announcement seems pointless; without it, however, he cannot retire, suitably, from the stage. The curtain cannot close upon him, for he comes to introduce the hieros, whom, he says, he "sees approaching." He cannot, like other deities, depart in a chariot, for, provided with wings, he is always represented, on sculptures and frescoes, as in flight, when in motion. He cannot ascend, as he has descended, by the graceful "trick" styled the "Descent of Mercury," as well known to modern acrobats as it was to ancient. "Per catadromum decucurrit." *Suet. in Neron.; Comment. Casaubon,* "Actionibus emptus, servus qui per catadromum descenderet." *Burmann,* A.D. 1756.

79 "It was the 'tamias'' duty to see the temple decorated." *Potter.* This was a festal day, 420. "The doors of churches, on fête days, are adorned with festoons of flowers." *Picart, Rel. Cer. Gr. Christ.* At line 55 the "hieros" is styled the "tamias."

83 "Earth," the western horizon. "Urge;" see 1150, 1151 and note.

85 Nûx was the ancient deity of night.

86 "The principal peak of Parnassos is 8000 ft. high, and even in modern times has been rarely reached; its glaciers being nearly perpendicular, its ascent is extremely dangerous." *Murray's Hand-book, Greece.*

88 Delphi, situated in a hollow, amongst mountains overtopped by the peaks of Parnassos, faced the east; hence these peaks were illumined by the rays of the rising sun, while plains and valleys, there, remained in twilight.

89 "Smûrnê," signifies incense, which was so called, not because the odoriferous resins grew at Smyrna, but because traders brought them there from the east. Thus we speak of "Turkey" rhubarb, because it was formerly purchased in Constantinople, though produced, exclusively, in China. Smurnê is improperly rendered as myrrh, an ingredient only in incense; Plutarch says a fifth part only. It is called, in the text, "dry," in contradistinction to liquid toilet preparations of it. "Capillos crispatos calido ferro, myrrhâque madentes."

92 The prophetess, in the crypt, amidst a rising vapour, hears the oracular words

which she repeats to the chief priests, who versify them, that she may, in due time, communicate them to votaries, in such sense as may suit their purpose.

95 The fountain of the nymph Castalia flowed into three tanks hewn in the rock, to serve as baths, respectively, for the priests, priestesses, and therapes. Votaries, before consulting the oracle, sprinkled themselves with its water, to which the Romans attributed sundry marvellous virtues. "This celebrated source was closed and diverted by an earthquake, A.D. 1870." *Murray.* "They attach a sanctity to certain fountains, which they look upon as miraculous waters." *Picart, Gr. Christians.* "The water from holy pools and wells finds a ready sale, when bottled." *Croker's Ireland.* "In Ireland votive offerings are suspended on trees surrounding holy wells." *Hall.*

101 Coarse language and blasphemy were not only considered unpolite, but as indicating evil omens, at ancient Athens, where euphemism was much in vogue. A dead person was spoken of as "one who had departed;" a prison as "a retreat," &c. *Paul's Greece.*

102 "Those who aspire to the priesthood are admitted, as novices, at ten years of age, and are immediately employed upon menial offices, by way of probation." *Picart, Gr. Christians.*

104 "Laurus nobilis," the "sweet bay." "Daphnê" was sacred to Apollo, because, after his futile pursuit of the nymph Daphnê, who was changed into that plant, he crowned himself with its leaves. The hieros alludes to the shrubs consecrated by the priests, which he alone, as Daphnephoros, was permitted to touch. By Catholics it is deemed sacrilege for a layman to touch the consecrated vessels.

105 "All who entered the Delphik temple asperged themselves with holy water from a tank in the cella, supplied by the Castalian fount." *Potter.* The survival of this custom in Christendom is remarkable.

106 In A.D. 1885, the military chapel at Aldershott had to be cleared of birds by rifle volleys, and at Sutton, Leicester, the parish church was closed for a fortnight, owing to an incursion of swallows.

108 "Anathemata," gold armour, tripods, craters, and jewels, suspended on bullæ, "roptra," bosses affixed to the antæ and brazen doors. *Smith, C. D.*

"Sur la place Saint Etienne étaient alignées quantité de boutiques en plein vent où se débitent, à la fête de Sainte Geneviève, patronne de Paris, des cierges, des chapelets, des figurines en cire, des médailles et autres offrandes votives." *Siége de Paris. Wey.* A.D. 1871.

112 Laurel cuttings, planted in vases in the temple courts at nightfall, when consecrated, became well-grown shrubs on the following morning. *Potter.* " At Naples, until a few years ago, an image of the Madonna was shaved in public, at stated periods, between each of which its hair was believed to be miraculously renewed." *Clemmens.*

116 From the vale of Tempê the Daphnephoros replenished the laurel and myrtle plantations in the Delphik sanctuary. He cut the shrubs, attended by a procession of priests and townspeople, with bands of music ; and, at night, the town was illuminated; and all the boys were crowned with wreaths of the sweet bay. *Smith, C. D.* " In the vale of Tempê countless rills, from the ever-melting snow on the mountain tops, water luxuriant forests of myrtle, laurel and blossoming shrubs which still perennially flourish, as gaily as they did three thousand years ago." *Dodwell.*

120 "Mursinê" was a name of Aphrodite, and of the myrtle sacred to her, and with which brides were crowned.

123 " The temple, built on a slope of the Phædriades' peak which faced the south, had a long period of sunlight." *Murray.*

124 " Paiân," a name of Apollo, as the archer who shoots and smites, and as deity of the Sun, whose rays shoot and heal. Pœan also signifies a hymn.

125 "Euaiôn eiên," a blest eternity be thine. " Blessed be our God, now and ever, and to the ages of ages ! " *Div. Lit. St. Chrysost.* " Glory to God, for ever and ever ! " Eis tous aiônas. *Apoc.* 7. 12. The priests, during each of the nine parts of their service, chant the *trisagium,* Holy God, holy and eternal, holy omnipotent, three times successively." *Picart, Gr. Christ.* " Holy, holy, Lord God Almighty ! " *Hymn, A. C.* " Seven times a day will I praise the Lord ! " *Psalms.*

129 As the prophetess announced the oracles of Apollo from his fane at Delphi, so did the Pontifex Maximus the presages of Deus Aius locutius from his temple on the Mons Vaticanus at Rome ; and so, from his palace on the same spot, does Papa Pontifex Maximus issue his bullæ.

130 " I will praise thee, O Lord my God, I will glorify thy name for evermore ! I had rather be a doorkeeper in the house of my God, &c. Praise him in his name Jah ! " *Psalms.*

137 By the use of the " omega " of Barnes, and insertion of a d' after " pateros," may this line in the text be made to tally with its fellow in the strophe ? It ought not to stand as it does, for the laws of musical progression prove it to be unrythmical.

138 " In the adytum was a gold statue of the God." *Dodwell.* Paley observes that the boy evinces his love for his God by the frequent repetition of his name, " Phoibos."

148 " Cleanse our souls and bodies from all pollution of the flesh and spirit, and vouchsafe unto us to stand blameless and uncondemned before thy holy altar." *Div. Lit. St. Chrysost.* See *Levit.* 15. 16. The chaste conduct of a Roman Catholic priest is certified, in a Latin document, on his leaving a diocese, by his bishop.

150 " One thing have I desired of the Lord, that I may dwell in the house of my Lord all the days of my life." *Psalms.*

152 To translate "agatha moira " as "good fortune," spoils the prayer ; " moira " means "part" as well as " lot." " Mary has chosen the good part ; " "agathên merida." *Luke* 11. 42. " Moira " and " meris " are "synonymous." *Brasse.* See Eum. Eschyl. 45, for a similar sense. Hieros alludes to his eligibility for the priesthood,

153 " Eâ," an ejaculation commonly used in Spain. *Lat. Eja. Fr.* " *Tiens.*"

154 " Vultures and eagles still build their nests in the rocks of Parnassos, and hover over the valleys." *Murray, H. B.* A.D. 1874.

155 Attracted by the odour of blood from slaughtered animals, birds of prey habitually infested temples' precincts.

157 *Pindar, Puth.,* speaks of " Phoibos' golden house," and later writers describe the " golden house of Nero," and the " gold temple of Umritsar."

158 Aquila chrysäeta, the golden eagle, bore Zeus' thunderbolts.

163 Scarlet (phenician), formerly called purple ; a mixture of red and yellow, is the colour of the unripe fruit of the Phœnix, palm, the date. See *Aulus Gellius,* and his statement confirmed by *Figuier,* in his *monde vegetal.*

165 Barnes fancies here a concetto on the strings of the lyre and bow, of both of

which Apollo was the inventor. " The bow string was made of horse-hair."
*Potter.*

167 In the tank, Trochoeides, in the island of Delos, were maintained the swans
sacred to Apollo. Kuknos, a son of that God, was metamorphosed into one of
those birds.

168 Aristotle having declared that swans sang well, and best when dying, Ælianus,
and certain modern naturalists, closely watched them, and came to the conclusion that the Stagyrite was a " gobe-mouches." They could have heard only
the harsh " whoop" of the Cycnus cantor, the whistling swan ; the chirp of
the Cycnus nigra collis is soft and sweet, resembling the subdued tone of a
clarionet.

171 The swallow, which the Hieros sees for the first time in the year, is introduced,
appropriately, during the Delphinia, the festival of Apollo, held at the vernal
equinox, in the month Monouchion, March, when that bird arrives, and
emigrates in September. "The settling of a swallow portended an evil omen."
*Potter.*

175 "Alpheus' river, meeting the Eurôtas, plunges into a chasm, then emerges and
sinks again." *Dodwell.* " Œstuat Alpheus." *Ovid.* At a distance, the boy
cannot determine the species of the swallow, whether it is the " hirundo
riparia," which dives beneath the water, or the " hirundo silvestris," which
inhabits the woods.

176 " Isthmus of Corinth." " At the southern foot of the Acro-Corinth, through
some thick and difficult forests of shrubs we proceeded." *Dodwell.*

180 Tablets, pretended missives from the Gods, were brought by carrier-pigeons.
In London, now, Tyrolese peasants tell fortunes by means of birds, who
present with their beaks tiny printed packets to the credulous.

183 It was the office of Hieros, as hospitaller, to receive pilgrims. 646.

184 The scribes, who have assigned the following speeches by women to the Khoros
generally, must have meant that members of that company entered on the
scene, to take part in the dialogue, and inspect the sculptures on the temple
frieze. That the number of such persons did not exceed two, the rule of the
Greek theatre (that more than three actors must not continue to speak in the
same dialogue, in a serious drama,) demonstrates. The stage, though extensively

long, was so narrow, that a Khoros, however small, could not have performed its evolutions thereon, and, on that account, throughout a play, it occupied the orchestra platform, on which a thymelè was placed for the especial purpose of the Khoreutes dancing round it, for all their dances were circular.

186 " At Delphi were 3000 statues." *Potter.* "Pliny asserts that many worshipped the shrined statues in the streets, and that all, who passed them, saluted them by kissing their hands to them." *Smith, C. D.* " Many Roman Catholics, now, cross themselves at sight of a sacred image." *Picart.*

189 At Delphi, to Artemis, " Letô's daughter" was a white marble temple with two pedimented porticoes, unusual at Athens then. See 465.

192 " The tasteless practice of tinting and bedizening marble statues obtained even in the time of Pericles." *Linton's Greece.* "Scimitars were used by the inhabitants of Argos, of which country Heracles was a native." *Potter.* The anachronism, by which that hero is introduced at a period antecedent to his birth, has been much dilated on. Euripides, however, does not describe the temple of Iôn's age, but that of his own, and he could not have done other-wise, for it was represented on the scene.

197 This woman had worked tapestry with Kreousa. 747. Thus mediæval châtelaines employed their damsels; Queen Matilda assisted in the Bayeux manufacture, personally.

198 Iolâus cauterized the necks of the Hydra, whose heads his chief had amputated. The last act of Garibaldi, "preux chevalier, sans peur et sans reproche," was to introduce a measure into the Italian Senate to drain the Pontine marshes. His great prototype cleared the pools of the pestilent swamps of Lerna, and suffocated their water snakes with sulphur.

201 Bellerophon, mounted on Pegasus, slays the Chimæra. At the Abbeville Cathedral is a stuffed crocodile, popularly known as "the dragon slain, by the Seigneur Dieudonné de Bozon, in the Holy Land." *Kitto, B. E.*

208 The statues in the pediment were entire; those on the outer frieze in alto-relievo. For battles of angels and giants, see *Genes.* 6. 4; *Apocal.* 12. 7; *Book of Enoch* 4. 10, *and passim.* In the museum at Berlin are the best metopes of " gigantomachia," so common on Greek temples.

209 The Greek k, before the vowels e and i, is pronounced, by the civilized

Spaniards, Italians, Poles, Germans, French and English soft, respectively, as th, ch, cz, ts, c; the barbarous Celts and hybrid Levantines all pronounce it as a hard k. Encelados was slain by Zeus.

211 "The Athenians had dedicated a new portico at Delphi, in return for Phormio's naval victory off Rhion." *Paley.* The women recognize these subjects as being the same as those embroidered on the Panathenaic " peplos," offered every fifth year to Pallas, at Athens. So at present, the " mantello" of Santa Rosalia at Palermo, the " vela " of Santa Agata at Catania, the " basquiña," worked by Ferdinand the Seventh for Madoña de Atocha, Nuestra Señora de la Soledad, at Madrid, the " saint suaire " at Cadouin, and the " heilige Kleid" at Trier, are all exhibited, at stated intervals, for the edification of the faithful.

212 A bolt lighted at both ends.

217 Bromios; Bacchus was called by the Làtins " imbellis," because his victories in India were bloodless. He never slew but by secondary means.

218 Horace says he killed Rhætus with his thyrsus. The names of six giants are recorded as slain by Bacchus.

220 Visitors, now, enter Turkish mosques, and oriental palaces and temples, on bared feet, " All persons remove their shoes, before entering Coptic Christian Churches." *Lane's Modern Egyptians.*

224 To touch the sacred laurel was to commit sacrilege; to gaze on the Gorgon was to be petrified, or burnt. Here was a warning to thieves! " The ' omphalos,' the entrance to the treasury of the temple, was covered by a white stone, on which were sculptured fabulous images." *Strabo.* " The omphalos was in the Aduton." *Diodorus.* Gold, to a fabulous amount, in vessels, statues and ingots, it is said, was presented to the Delphic temple by Gyges, Crœsus and Gorgias.

225 The boy speaks from report only; not being a priest, he had never entered the crypt. 414. 1362. "According to the ritual of the Greek Christian Church, the priesthood, alone, enters the sanctuary, which is divided from the nave by a screen. Its doors are called the holy gates." *Anastasius, Hope,* 24, 338.

226 Cakes, as minor offerings, were burnt upon the altars; salted, or mixed with honey or conserves, they were moulded in the forms of sacrificial victims. In

such shapes, now, on fête days, in Spain, people offer them to friends and even strangers. The Jews offered cakes to Javeh. *Lev. 7*; *Numbers, 15*.

228 The altar in the court before the portico. "Women were not admitted inside temples." *Potter.* "In certain cases, churches are closed to women, but they may stand outside them." *Picart Chris. Greeks.* Until quite lately women were not admitted into Jewish synagogues. "From all Roman Catholic monasteries, except refuges, they are still excluded, unless provided with the papal brevet." *Murray.*

229 The regulations as prescribed for males.

230 Both women know that they cannot enter the nave. The elder apologizes for the impertinence of the younger, who resembles certain persons who, now, try the patience of guides by asking them absurd questions. See *Longfellow's Hyperion*, and *Clemmens' Pilgrims*.

233 "Guala," the adytum, crypt. The girl tells a falsehood in order to exasperate the hieros.

234 The hospitaller fulfils his office rudely. The rhymes stand as in the original text.

239 Only the working classes, now, have this diagnosis.

245 Apollo could not endure gloomy faces in his courts; at his sacred isle, Delos, none were permitted to be sick or sorry, least of all to die. *Athenæus and Lucian.* Louis the Fourteenth, who assumed the God's title of "Le Roy Soleil," shared his opinion, and the late Duke of Nassau, who inscribed, in gold letters, on the arch at Wiesbaden, "Curis vacuus, adeas hunc locum," seems to have entertained similar sentiments. "Enter into his gates with thanksgiving—ye shall rejoice before your God." *Deut. 12. 12.* Amongst several inscriptions on the architraves of the Delphik temple, were the maxims of the seven sages of Greece, and that of "gnôthi seauton." "Fragments of inscribed stones are numerous amongst its ruins." *Dodwell.*

256 She means that her complaints are useless.

258 He enquires in his official capacity, as hospitaller.

265 As a student, he seeks information on disputed historical subjects.

268 She means that her noble birth has not protected her from outrage, and that she is without an heir.

269 Athene was present at the miracle worked by Hephaistos. See note 21. These questions refer to the sculptures on the western pediment of the Parthenon. Note 49.

271 Hence, it would appear that the Hellenic children received instruction from graphic illustrations, as all European do at present.

272 See 22.

274 Pallas, hearing that her orders had been disobeyed, smote with madness the girls, who flung themselves from the rocks. Note 23.

278 Orithia, Procris, and Othonia were slain by their father, to whom the oracle had promised a victory, if he did so. Compare with this story that of Jepthah. *Judges*, 11. 31. Erectheus died 1347 B.C. *Bell.* Jepthah ruled 1253 B.C. *Hales.*

282 Erectheus had killed, in battle, Eumolpos, son of Poseidôn. That God was styled the " Earth-shaker." Kreousa means that an earthquake was the cause of her father's death, of which, however, historians vary in their accounts.

284 See 502.

285 "Astrapai" are rendered by commentators as "lightnings;" but over them none but Zeus had control. On bas reliefs, gems and frescoes, Apollo is represented both with a disc and rays of light round his head, precisely as Christian saints have been depicted. The God had a temple at Athens, called Puthion. " Apollo chrysocomes cognominatur, a fulgore radiorum quos vocant comas aureas solis." *Macrob. Sat. l.* 1, *c.* 17. "Genitor, circum caput omne, micantes deposuit radios." *Ov. Met.* 1. 2. 40.

286 This allusion to Apollo's rays angers Kreousa. 888.

293 " Marriage of an Athenian with an alien was illegal. This law, which had become obsolete, was revived, annulled, and renewed in the time of Pericles." *Potter.*

295 The straits of Euripos, over which the first bridge was erected in Euripides' time.

300 The excavated temple of the seer Trophonios, the deified architect of the Delphik fane, was at Libadia, in Bœotia, fifty-five miles from Athens, and fifteen from Delphi. At some point where the roads diverged, Kreousa had separated from Xouthos, and proceeded on her journey. "The Trophonion cave, of which no trace remains, was visited by pilgrims, before consulting

Apollo's oracle, in the hope that, if one response were obscure, the other might be explicit." *Smith.*

301 " Pausanias says that Libadia was one of the most ornamented towns in Greece." *Dodwell.*

303 The barren land and the barren womb were the dreaded calamities of a princely family. " The horse-leech hath two daughters, &c." *Prov.* 30. 15. " Horse-leech, *alukah*, arabic, fate." *Kitto.*

310 " At Delphi was an important slave market." *Smith.*

311 Loxiou Kouros, as Castor and Pollux were styled Dioskouroi.

315 See 56. During the Middle Ages, "the sacristan slept in the nave of a Christian church, as its principal custodian, in a special niche." *The Builder,* *St. Albans Abbey, Cutts.*

320 See 1492.

323 See 52, and note 183.

329 " Phew " is a common ejaculation in Ireland.

335 " At Delphi, each Greek tribe was represented by a Proxenos, who, as a consul, supplied visitors with information, and recommended them to hotels and lodging-houses. Unless introduced by this official, none could consult the oracle." *Potter.*

337 " Aidôs " was the Deity of Shame and Reserve. Kreousa, ashamed to tell her story, alludes to the Goddess's first attribute ; Hieros fancies that she does so to her second, and informs her that, as the God knows all her thoughts, it is useless for her to attempt to conceal them from him. " Hieromonachos says to a novice, We are in the presence of the Angel of the Lord, before whom we must not presume to tell lies, nor to have any mental reservation." *Picart.* *Christ. Greeks.*

339 Evidently, the pious young sacristan has been properly kept in ignorance of the impure stories of the "Loves of the Gods," for he discredits Kreousa's tale, and is shocked at its blasphemy.

" Sumserit annales, nihil est hirsutius illis :
facta sit unde parens Ilia nempe leget."

*Ov. Trist.* 2. 259. *Comm. Passer.*

" Annales maximos, pontificum operâ confectos." " Hirsutius libidinosius interpretatur." Roman Catholic priests permit their flock to read only such passages in the Old Testament as their Church has selected for the perusal of the laity.

342 In the word "suffered" Kreousa hints at the rape; but the boy misses the *double entente.*

348 Wolves, lynxes and boars infested the district.

354 By the word "Hêbê" it is signified that the hieros is "ephebos," æt. 16. *Brumoy, Théâtre de la Grèce.*

366 Tacitus speaks of the Delphik tripod as "common to the human race." As the Sun, on Egyptian cartouches, is the emblem of truth and justice, so is Apollo as Deity of that luminary. "Solem quis dicere falsum audeat?" *Vir. Geor. 2.*

375 "If the entrails were healthy, the omen was considered favourable, if diseased, unfavourable." *Potter.* "Christian Greeks examine fibres of bones at meals, in order to presage fortunes, and Pennant, in his tour in the Scotch highlands, mentions the observance there of a somewhat similar custom." *Dodwell.*

380 See *Juvenal's tenth satire's* conclusion, and *Luke,* 12. 20. 30.

381 "Pourquoi, dans ce globe, un destin trop fatal pour une once de bien, mit cent quintaux de mal?" *Les Systemes. Voltaire.*

384 Without the intervention of the priests, Kreousa accomplishes her object of questioning the God, before her spouse arrives. 334. The sacristan is shocked at her audacity and impiety.

390 "The Lord hath hid it from me, and hath not told me." *Kings,* 2. 4. 27.

391 The oracle of Zeus at Dodona.

403 Pausanias speaks of the tedious ceremonials attendant upon a visit to Trophonios' cave.

413 At certain temples, the oracles were reported by the hospitaller. "Ædituus responsa numinis sui prædicat." *Macrob. Sat. l.* 2. 2. 3. Xouthos perceives that the Hieros is that official.

414 The "Hosioi," five in number, were elected, by lot, by the priests of the sacred college at Delphi, as the Pope is by the cardinals of that of Rome. "The names of certain priests, amongst the Christian Copts, are written on slips of paper, which are rolled into balls and deposited in a receptacle. He whose name is drawn is invited to assume the office of Patriarch, when vacant." *Lane's Modern Egyptians.*

419 " On certain days, during the Puthion festival, oracles were proclaimed, in public, in the pronaos." *Potter.*

420 " Tablets, notifying auspicious and inauspicious days, were suspended on public buildings." *Potter.* " The day sacred to Apollo was his natal day (Sunday). *Hesiod Er.* 3, 105. " The evening and the morning were the first day." *Gen.* I. Solis dies, Sunday, Sonntag, Zoon-dag; Baal, the Lord, the Sun; Baal-zeveen, the Sun's day, the Lord's day: Kuriaka Hêmera, Dies Dominicalis, Domenica, Domingo, Dimanche. See *Gibbon, D. & F. c.* 20. " The Sun's day, that upon which the Creator changed darkness to light, and upon which the Saviour rose from death to life." *Justin Martyr,* A.D. 140.
Paley quotes Æschyl. Theb. where the seventh day of the month is mentioned as sacred to Apollôn Hebdomagades, but Liddell says that such institution obtained only in Sparta.

421 Xouthos wishes to make his application before the crowd assembles. " As a person of distinction, he was entitled to the Promanteia, precedence at the oracle, and a special communication therefrom." *Smith, C. D.*

422 In the peristyle of a Greek temple, dedicated to a particular God, were shrines and statues to other Gods, as, in a Roman Catholic church, dedicated to a particular Saint, are shrines and statues to other saints. " If the ancient Greeks had a hundred Gods, the modern Greeks have a hundred Saints." *Hope's Anastasius.*

> " Il faut pourtant en faire différence,
> Un Saint vaut mieux que tous les Dieux payens."
> *La Pucelle. Voltaire.*

423 Laurel and palm branches were carried by suppliants at shrines. These boughs were sold at the temples, as willow branches for Palm Sunday, and wax candles are for offerings, in Roman Catholic churches.

426 See 356. The advent of a son by Xouthos, owing to the intercession of Apollo, would not compensate Kreousa for the loss of her child by that God, and for his outrage upon her.

429 Kreousa's irreverence at the shrine convinces the hieros that she has not come to question the oracle. He discredits all her statements, which he considers pretexts to veil the real object of her visit, consultation with the secular Delphik authorities, upon important Athenian interests.

435 The tank in the pronaos. Note 105. "Before a sacrifice, holy water was sprinkled about the cella and vestibule, and over the worshippers." *Potter.* "In Catholic churches, before high mass, an acolyte, preceded by the crucifix bearer, carries the holy water-pail, whose contents the priest scatters with an aspersorium." *Picart. Rel. Cer.*

436 The scribes have been in error assigning this speech to Iôn, an important official at the temple, who, ignorant of the tales of the "Loves of the Gods" (339), never falters in his allegiance to Apollo, and faith in the religion which he professes. What follows is totally inconsistent with all which he has hitherto expressed.

440 This passage has attracted much attention. Terence, in his Eunuchus, quotes Ennius upon its subject. It has been eulogized by St. Cyprian and Justin Martyr, and Grotius especially refers to it.

445 "The fine for violating a virgin was a thousand drachma." *Solon. Potter.*

453 Aneileithuiê, a term applicable to a virgin, as one who has not needed the assistance of Eileithuiâ, the Deity who presides over child-birth.

455 Promêtheus-Titânos, the provident Titan, Hephaistos, not the son of Iapetos and Klumenê. *Lucian. Dial.* 8.
The sculptures in the eastern pediment of the Parthenon are here alluded to. *Pausan. I. 24. 5*
"This temple dedicated to the virgin Deity Pallas, after the introduction of Christianity, was rededicated to the Blessed Virgin Mary." *Guide to the Elgin room, Brit. Mus.* 1880, A.D.

460 In *Eum. Æsch.* 404, Pallas is styled "wingless," and arrives in a car, as in this play (1570), but a statue of her, as the winged Nîcê, stood in the western pediment of the Parthenon.

465 Lêtô's daughter, Artemis, had a temple at Delphi. 188.

466 The damsels invoke the virgin deities as their patronesses.

468 To whom were the Goddesses to pray? The Moirai were influenced only by Anangkê, who was never supplicated, for she had neither priests nor altars. Æschylus' Electra calls upon Hermes to summon the infernal Deities, and Gaia, to hear her orisons, and invokes her deceased father. See the Catholic prayers for intercession. *Litanies of the Saints, of the dying, for the faithful departed. Golden Manual, Burns,* 1850, A.D.

478 " Legitimate children inherited their parents' property by right, and, not until the laws of Solon were promulgated, could testamentary wills be made to their detriment." *Potter.*

484 "As arrows are in the hands of a mighty man, so are children of youth. Happy is the man who hath his quiver full of them, they shall not be ashamed, when they meet their enemies in the gate." Or, "shall not be dismayed, but subdue their enemies in the gate." *Kitto. Psalm* 127.

492 " Pân was one of the deities who presided over child-birth." *Athenæus.* Kreousa decorates his altar, as she has promised Xouthos. 424. Pân had a rock-cut temple at Makrai, for a description of the ruins of which, see *Dodwell's Greece,* I. 304.

493 The rock on which stood the Parthenon.

494 "Caves, natural and artificial, are numerous on the Athenian hills." *Murray.*

496 " Agraulis had a shrine at Makrai." *Williams' Greece.*

500 From this passage we learn that the Khoros performed its odes to suit the different sentiments expressed therein : the metres were changed, and the musical strains modulated into different keys. "For you, ô Bacchus, do we now set forth the tuneful song, uttering, in various melody, the simple rythm." *Samos the Delian. Athenæus B.* 14. *c.* 15.

502 " Miltiades placed a colossal Parian marble statue of Pân in his rock-cut temple at Athens." *Dodwell.*

503 In one of the caves of Makrai. See 17, and note. The faulty construction of this passage Aristophanes has ridiculed in *Lysis.* 911.

507 " The sons of Olympian Gods, by mortal females, were persecuted during their lives, and perished by violent deaths." *Tooke's Pantheon.*

510 Had not Hieros been absent from his post of Ædituus, he would not have asked if Xouthos had quitted the temple, for it was his business, as Tamias, to receive the fees from that prince, and, as hospitaller to take leave of him. Xouthos has been disappointed of his private oracle before the sacrifice (419), and has been detained until the conclusion of the ceremonies, consequently has only just received it. We may suppose that he has been purposely delayed, in order that he may meet the Hieros, on his return to the temple.

That pageants and dances were introduced during the interludes of a Greek drama is notorious. Pindar, *Puth.* 4, speaks of the " edifying processions of

Apollo" at his festivals. In the sixteenth and seventeenth centuries, the *intermezzi* and interludes, at the Italian and French theatres, were unconnected with the plots of plays. In the early English drama, dumb show frequently occurs, as an integral part of stage business, between the acts. Beaumarchais observes that, "to maintain the interest of a serious piece, pantomime, appropriate to the subject of its intrigue, should fill up the pauses consequent upon its entractes." *Beaumarchais, " Eugenie,"* 1762 A.D.

512 The tripod in the nave, not crypt. See note 92.

519 " The Papa's daughter-in-law, on entering the room, kissed her own hand, saying, Sas proskûnô. A salutation of this kind denotes the greatest respect; it is an ancient custom." *Dodwell's Greece,* 1. 169. Hope, in his Anastasius, speaks of the Turkish pachas as being saluted in a similar manner by the modern Greeks. " Cæcilius, manum ori admovens, osculum labiis pressit." *Minucius Felix.* " Jactat basia tibicen, gratulari fautores putat." *Phædrus,* 5. 7.

520 The Gods inflicted mania on mortals with whom they were offended. " Hon theos thelei apolesai, prôt' apophrenei." *Eur. Frag.* "Quem Jupiter vult perdere prius dementat." See the story of Nebuchadnezzar, *Kings,* 2. 25, and St. Jerome's comment thereon.

522 The hieros wears a wreath of consecrated laurel, similar to that on Apollo's statue. See 104 and note.

527 Xouthos alludes to the funeral pyre. " A son was bound by law to attend his father's obsequies." *Potter.*

536 Xouthos, by interpreting the response according to his wishes, deceives himself (825) and causes the Hieros mental distress (1525). For Phoibos' words see 787.

542 From the boy's sarcastic question, and Xouthos' rough rejoinder, we may be led to suppose that Kreousa's family legend was credited only by Athenians.

549 A seventy miles' journey, if from Athens; seventy-five, if from Chalcis, the scene of Xouthos' triumph, and forty-five, if from Achaia, his native country.

550 The festival of Dionûsos lasted, annually, from the 15th of March to the 1st of April. It was celebrated for its rites, entertainments, fairs and torch processions. In Catholic countries, and their colonies, Carnivals are held before Lent. Modern Greeks, also, keep the Carnival. *Dodwell.*

551 Proxenos, see note 335. Delphik women of the town, not temple.

553 The respectable priestesses of Dionusos (see Demosth: Or: Nic :) should not be confounded with the Mænads, priestesses *pour rire*, harlots of the town, engaged for the processions, inebriated, semi-nude, ivy-crowned, flaunting leopard-hides on their shoulders, brandishing torches and thyrsi, and reeling, rather than dancing, through the streets, yelling Evöe. "Men, by whom they wished to be followed, they struck with their thyrsi; those who declined to do so received from them further strokes." *Dodwell.* We are here reminded of the " Descente de la Courtille," after the procession of the " Bœuf-gras" and the carnival balls at Paris.

> " Mais du Temple voici la fête !
> Voici la nuit du Bacchanal,
> et tout Paris, gaiement, s'apprète
> a nous payer son Carnaval ! " *Fils du diable. Féval.*

554 " 'Tis the received opinion of physicians that none but puling chits and booby fools are procreated in drunkenness." *Amphytrion, Dryden.*

556 " As a foundling, unclaimed by a freeman, such would have been, legally, his condition." *Potter.*

562 See 421 and note.

574 The gallant soldier wishes to be assured of the welfare of her whom he supposes the mother of his child.

576 The office of Daphnephoros was necessarily of limited duration; for it could be held, only, by a boy.

589 The humble, and the three subdivisions of the noble class, are here alluded to.

595 The idea of a person entering a trireme, or theatre, is here suggested,

603 " The metoikoi, sojourners, enjoyed a limited liberty at Athens, but, to acquire the freedom of the city, the majority of the ' bean-votes ' of 6000 burghers was requisite." *Potter.* An illegitimate son of an alien could not have obtained that honour.

613 Throughout Europe, on state occasions, younger children of royal families sit at the throne's foot ; the crown prince, on a low chair, on the right hand of the sovereign. " The subsellium, stool of honour." *Il corricolo, c.* 13, *Dumas.* Kreousa would have bitterly gazed on her son's empty seat.

617 "An epidemic of husband-poisoning has broken out in Slavonia." *Pesth, Dec.* A.D. 1888. *Standard.*

628 "No art, no letters, and no society, but a continuous fear and danger of a violent death." *Hobbes of Malmesbury.* "The Emperor of Russia lives secluded, and sees none but flatterers around him. . . . . Another attempt to assassinate him is reported on the Bourse." *Vienna, Dec.* 1887. *Standard.*

631 "Where your treasure is, there will your hearts be also." *Matt.* 6.

632 "Give me neither poverty nor riches, feed me with food convenient for me." *Proverbs* 30.

636 Here is an allusion to unmannered boors who, in a crowded thoroughfare, push their fellow passengers, from the footway, into the cart-road.

639 See note 245.

640 As hospitaller, and receiver of pilgrims. See note 51. Also *Hom. Od.* 15. 75, and *Pope's translation.*

643 As a foundling, left at the temple gates, (556) devoted to the God. As delighting in his sacred office, 102.

644 The text at the commencement and the pious sentiment at the conclusion of this oration, interlarded with scholastic mottoes and trite proverbs, remind us that, in former times, "novices at monasteries preached homilies from pulpits." *Cutts' Middle Ages.*

652 The "Genethlia" were the rites at nativity. Ten days after a child was born, sacrifices were offered to its Daimôn Genethlion, the tutelar Deities of its family, and Genitulla. At a feast, in the presence of friends and relatives, the infant received its name, and, unless these ceremonies were registered, it could not inherit property. Childless persons could adopt heirs, and, when they did so, similar rites were indispensable. *Potter.* Hence, Hellenes and Romans celebrated their name-days as annual festivals, as do Christian Greeks and Roman Catholics of the Latin race, at present, noting their days of birth for legal purposes, only. New born infants are baptized, and anointed with the Chrism, as soon as convenient, and, in addition to names given to them, they receive those of the Saints to whom, in the calendar of the country to which they belong, the days of their christening are dedicated. Such Saints are claimed as the patrons of

the children during their lives. To this solemnity a banquet invariably succeeds.

668 Referring to the circumstances of his birth, he alludes to Xouthos' words, 579. 650.

672 "A son, though illegitimate, of an Athenian freewoman, inherited her privileges." *Potter.*

674 Symbols were sold to aliens, permitting them to dwell and trade, (in partnership with natives only,) in Athens, but they were not allowed to harangue in public, or plead in the law-courts, hence the Agora was excluded to them. *Potter.* Parchment scrolls, representing the freedom of the city, are delivered by the London corporation to Britons and naturalized foreigners, upon payment of fees.

678 "Turannos" signifies queen, as well as king.

686 Pupils at the Delphic college were taught to compose sentences in verse, so that they might convey opposite meanings; hence the Oracles "paltered in a double sense," as in the trite example "Aio te, Æacidas Romanos vincere posse," and in the death-warrant for Edward the Second, "Edwardum occidere nolite timere bonum est." See *Rabelais B.* 3. *c.* 19. "At present, the urn of Amorgos, at Mount Athos, does duty as an Oracle." *Picart, Greek Christ.*

701 "Men were obliged to cohabit with their wives, if heiresses, thrice a month." *Potter.*

702 Xouthos had been banished from his country by his brothers. *Smith, C. D.* See 1297, the "hired ally," the soldier of fortune.

707 The three ensuing lines, missing in the MSS., have been metrically suggested by Barnes.

717 Dionusos was believed to join in the dances round his altar. For a description of a Greek dance see *Homer, on the shield of Achilles*, and *Burton*, in his *Anatomy of Melancholy*, on the Greek gaillarde, from the spirited account of it by Apuleius.

721 The Coryphæus enrages the women of the Chorus, by tauntingly reminding them that they gladly received an "alien" in Xouthos, when he came to aid them in their peril.

725 The paidagôgos was a servant, who acted as governor of the children in a

Hellenic family, but who was nowise concerned in their education. In France, even now, amongst opulent families, boys and girls under age are not allowed to leave home, unless accompanied by male or female domestics, or trusted friends.

727 Kreousa could not, herself, make the enquiry, females not being admitted into temples.

736 Only low-born, opulent people treat servants otherwise than well.

739 " The steps of the Parthenon perceptibly rise in the middle." *Westropp's Hand-book*. " The stairs, though horizontal, are slightly convex." *Bädecker— Athens*.

740 " The task of a physician is to relieve suffering." *Vossische Zeitung, Oct.* A.D. 1888.

743 The "sloping ground" must be imagined; there is no space for it on the scena.

747 See note 197.

756 See 667.

765 " Aiê," an ejaculation of distress, as common now in the Levant, as on the continent.

770 If she receive a message from her husband.

787 See Xouthos' misinterpretation of the oracle, 536. The maid must have been informed of its exact words, while in the peristyle, 675, 746, for Pallas, 1561, and Kreousa, 1534, recite them to the same effect.

796 " Oh that I had wings like a dove, then would I flee away and be at rest." *Psalm* 55.

797 Beyond the pillars of Hercules, (straits of Gibraltar,) the limits of the earth were supposed; the sun was invisible, and, in airy space, lighted only by stars, in proximity were the Hesperides, the isles of the blest, (Fortunate isles) the western region, the asylum of the righteous, after death, for which Kreousa longs, 763.

798 Kreousa, judging from Iôn's age, 354, fancies that Xouthos' infidelity is of long standing.

805 In the temple courts, note 1130.

821 " Babes, dedicated to God by early Christians, were deposited in cradles upon principal altars of churches." *Cutts' Middle Ages*.

824 Presbus is, as yet, unaware that Kreousa needed no persuasion, 332.

839 Xouthos' child, born before his marriage with Kreousa.

842 The sons of Xouthos' brothers. "If an heiress cannot conceive children by her husband, she may seek an heir amongst the nearest of his relations." *Plutarch, from Solon.*

852 For a similar passage see *Eurip. Hel.* He knows that he must be slain if he murders Iôn. His "patrons" he considers Erektheus, his queen, and Kreousa.

856 But Homer says, "On the day when man becomes a slave, he loses half his manly virtues." *Gibbon, D. F. c. 57.* "Makes man a slave, takes his worth away." *Athen. Deip. B. 6. c. 87.* Another author, however, has "Doulos Epiktêtos . . . . philos athanatois." *Epitaphs.*

858 "It is better to perish in honour, than to live on in shame!" *Von Bismarck's speech to the Reichstag, Jan. 13, 1886.*

859                     "O Heart, o heavy Heart,
                        why sigh'st thou without breaking?—
                   Because thou can'st not ease thy smart
                        with Friendship, nor by speaking." *Shakes. Troil.*

"Conquerar, an taceam?" *Ovid.* "Eloquar, an sileam?" *Virg.* Kreousa feels compelled to reveal her secret. Her declaration to Athenians that she has a son, though illegitimate, of whose whereabouts she is ignorant, but of whose death she has had no official notice, will debar a son of Xouthos from ascending the throne of Attica. See Pallas' opinion thereon, 1574.

871 The statue of Athênê-polias-promachos is here alluded to, as guard. The acropolis had but one entrance.

872 Tritônia was a name of Pallas. Is the Libyan, or the Hellenic Tritônis, here referred to?

884 The Cithara of Apollo was an open, harp-like instrument, whose yoke was composed of a pair of long hollowed cattle-horns, joined at the base which formed the sound-board; hence, his music may be said to proceed from "horns," but not from "horns through which he breathes." In the Museo Borbonico, at Naples, is a fresco from Herculaneum, on which Apollo is represented, seated on a hill, playing on the lyre and singing, surrounded by the nine Muses. *Ant. Herc. tom. 7.*

117

887 Glittering with his halo-rays. See note 285.

888 The hair of Apollo's statue was gilt. See note 192.

889 The swain Krokos was metamorphosed into the flower, " Crocus aureus, golden yellow, February, Greece." *Gard. Dict.* Its season shows that the babe was exposed to the cold of November.

890 " And winking mary-buds begin to ope their golden eyes !" *Shakespeare—Cymbelin.*

893 Maia, Demeter, whose daughter Kora was carried away by Pluto, while she was gathering crocuses. " Ipsa crocos tenues . . . legit . . . Illa quidem clamabat, Io, carissima mater, auferor !" *Ov. Fasti, l. 4.442.* The word "matèr," which Kreousa uses, cannot be meant to refer to her own mother, for, had Praxithea been close at hand, the outrage could not have been kept secret ; indeed, it could not have occurred. See 897.

895 Similar passages occur in modern French literature. " Son excellence . . . . se delaissait des soucis de la politique, en fètant Venus." *L'amant d'Alice, Montépin,* 1875 A.D.

909 " In the aduton of the Puthion temple at Delphi, was a statue of Apollo in solid gold." *Potter.*

919 She prophesies to the God the cessation of his cult in his sacred isle. She taunts him with his semi-mortal birth, and would degrade him to the rank of a Demigod ; sneering at his mother's deification, she alludes to the practice of women clutching at an adjacent object to assuage the pangs of child-birth, and she scoffs at the reverence paid to his favourite laurel.

920 The delivery of Lêtô, at Delos, having been difficult and protracted, the laurel and palm were miraculously created, that, by grasping them, she might receive assistance in her travail. *Ælianus l. 5. c. 4.* Anius displays to Eneas the marvels of the Delphic fane " Urbemq' ostendit, delubraque, vota, duasque Latonâ quondam stirpes pariente retentas." *Ov. Met.* 13. 4. See *Hec. Eur.* 458. *Iphig. Tau.* 1100. *Hes. Theog.* 15.

921 See *Exodus* 1-16, *and Comm: Lane's Modern Egyptians, v.* 2, 275, and *Hooper's Med. Dic. Partur.* Pliny asserts that the natives of Delos indicated a tall palm as the identical tree near which Phoibos and Artemis were born.

934 See note 859, l. 337, and note.

942 Observe that the old slave accepts the miraculous tale which the educated hieros rejects! 341.

944 Not the illness attending parturition, for from that Apollo had preserved her, 1595, but the nausea consequent on conception. See *Hooper's Med. Dict. Partur.*

949 A semicolon should be inserted after " alone," " monê," for see 14. 15. 17. 503. 900.

957 Atê and Harpocrates.

969 " Sooner or later, all things pass away and are no more." *Isabella. Sotherne.*
" So lehre sie das nichts bestehet, das alles Irdische verhallt." *Schiller. Lied von der Glocke.*

974 The Delphic fane had been frequently destroyed by fire. Without windows, and lighted by apertures in the roof, containing much drapery, and altars with flaming pyres, the temple could be easily ignited by an incendiary. " The church of the monastery, at Megaspelion, embellished with marbles, gilding, and paintings of Saints, is illuminated with silver lamps, but badly lighted from without." *Dodwell's Greece,* 2. 450.

979 That the gentle Kreousa should, so suddenly, become a murderess at heart may seem unnatural, but is not so. In A.D. 1885, at the Hague, during the trial of a woman for murder, it transpired that she had been violated in her youth. " The Judge ruled that a female, thus outraged, ought not to be held responsible for her actions, taking into consideration the moral and physical deterioration which must necessarily take place in her, and he sentenced the prisoner, though she was found guilty, only to be kept under permanent restraint." *Standard.*

988 Campus Phlegræus in Macedonia. See *Hamilton's Campi Phlegraei,* A.D. 1777, and *Dodwell's Greece,* 2. 128.

989 The Gorgon, daughter of Tartarus and Gaia, slain by Pallas, must not be confounded with one of the three Gorgons alluded to, 224, the daughters of Phorcys and Cêto.

996 The Aigis, the goat-skin breastplate and surcoat of Pallas, fringed with serpents, and covered with scales of the same.

1002 Kreousa hesitates, for she is aware that she is committing sacrilege by plotting murder in the temple courts, 1224.

1009 On poisoned bracelets, rings and necklaces of the 16th century, see *Crimes célèbres, Medicis, Dumas.*

1011 " The 'vena cava' conveys the blood from the liver to the heart." *Badham.*

1013 " On the Canterbury ampulla, believed to contain a drop of St. Thomas à Beckett's blood, mixed with water, whose touch was said to cure all diseases, was the following inscription: ' Optimus ægrorum medicus fit Thoma bonorum.' " See *Cutts' Middle Ages,* p. 171.

1017 Good and evil, being antagonistic, can neither amalgamate nor exist long together; as both are in created beings, Death may be the necessary consequence of their separation. See *Matthew,* 7. 12, and *Romans, St. Paul* 6.

1022 See 980, 851.

1024 " La position d'une belle mère est toujours suspecte." *La Marâtre. Balzac.*

1030 As many a godmother presents a silver cup to the infant which she holds at the baptismal font, so it appears that Pallas gave a gold ewer to Ericthonios, whom as a babe she raised from the ground. (269.) Kreousa must have had this vessel at her hotel, amongst other necessary "articles de voyage." At many inns in Spain travellers are still expected to bring with them all requisites for the " service de bouche," and provisions likewise.

1034 The disordered state of Kreousa's mind becomes now apparent. She proposes to slay the Hieros with poison poured from a vase, a sacred ancestral relic, into a holy libation. Her sin is as heinous as that of the monk who endeavoured to kill the Emperor Henry 7th with an envenomed sacramental wafer. Without evincing the least remorse, she orders her old and faithful slave to meet his immediate death.

1046 Buckle, in his *Civilization,* has proved, from statistics, that the number of murders rises and falls *pari passu* with the increase and decrease of population. In December, 1887, Sir T. Chambers, in his charge to a grand jury, observed: " Though many a crime has lately decreased, one, that of murder has remained stationary." *Standard.* " It must needs be that offences come "— ANAGKE estin. *Matthew* 18. 7.

1048 Einodiê (in the roads) Kora, (Demeter's, Maia's, daughter,) so called from her three-headed statue placed where three streets met. Representing three different personages, she was styled the three-formed goddess, potent on earth, in heaven and hell. She is here begged to guide, by her moon-light and illuminated altars in the streets, the old slave carrying the poisoned vase through the tortuous paths which lead up to the Delphic temple. In many continental cities statuettes of the blessed Virgin and the saints are placed at the corners of streets, where the lamplights from their miniature shrines prove serviceable to wayfarers.

1050 Poisonous herbs being supposed to be more efficacious when gathered by moonlight, Kora, in her character of Selênê, was believed to take an interest in venom.

1051 Hell-fiend, "Kthonias, infernal, katakthonias." *Greverus on Hesiod.*—Æschylus and Euripides call the Eumenides "Kthonias," and Homer and Virgil locate the Gorgon in the infernal regions.

1074 The God, Bakkhos, 717.

1075 Kallikhoros was a fountain at Eleusis, where the Dionysian orgies were held.

1076 The Eikadôn torch was the beacon lit on the twentieth day of the month Boedromion. On the 7th of August, the sixth day of the Eleusinian mysteries, the feast of Kora commenced, the ceremonies at which no alien was permitted to witness. Hone, in his "Day-book," furnishes an account of the bonfires, processions and pageants at the festival of St. John Baptist, in Great Britain, with a woodcut of an ancient beacon. See *Picart*, on the *Festa of St. Agatha at Catania*, and *Croker's Ireland*, 275.

1079 " The Cyclic dance originated from the belief that the heavenly bodies moved round the earth." *Francklin's Sophocles.* "Some say the Sun and Moon dance about the earth . . . the planets . . . and all belike to the music of the Spheres." *Burton, An. Mel., p. 3. S. 2.* See *Orchestra, Davies*, 1603 A.D. " Praise ye the Lord ; praise him ye stars of light ! Let them praise his name in the dance." *Psalm, 149. 158.*

1080 Selene, the moon, represented by Artemis as well as Kora. As Bakkhos led the dance in his honour, so did Kora in hers.

1081 The Nereides, the water nymphs, as the fifty Khoreutai. " Then shall the virgins rejoice in the dance." *Jer. 13.*

1082 " Ye elves, . . . and ye that on the sand, with printless foot, do chase the

ebbing Neptune, and do fly him when he comes back." *Shakespeare, Tempest,*
*A . 5. S. 1.*

1086 Maia, Demeter, Kora's mother. " The festivals of Ceres and Proserpina were
held at different periods in the year, the former at seed, and the latter at
harvest time." *Burmann on Ovid.*

1089 Iôn was about to resign his office at the temple.

1091 In the farces of the " middle comedy," the *" coureurs de femmes,"* and " *lorettes en
vogue,"* of the period, were scurrilously lampooned. None of these pieces are
extant entire, but fragments of them, suitable to illustrate this passage, are cited
by Athenæus, B. 13. c. 7. See line 398 here, and *Ovid. Met.* 3. 4.

1097 After the performance of the " Filles de marbre," at the Théâtre Vaudeville
at Paris, A.D. 1853, " *ces p'tites dames* " railed at its *collaborateurs,* and told them
that, as *femmes seules,* they could not be accused of adultery, of which many
of their patrons were guilty, and they boasted of their "piety" and regular
attendance at Mass.

1099 In allusion to Xouthos.

1106 In large households men-servants call waiting-women ladies.

1112 " Flung from a rock and stones thrown upon her." *Paley.* See Note 1223.

1113 " The attendants speak of their mistress's perilous condition as if it were their
own, as domestics in superior establishments identify themselves with the
affairs and property of their employers." *Barnes.* So also the Latin " servi,"
*Amph. Plaut. A . 3. S. 3.* So also the negroes in the United States, before their
emancipation. *Communicated by W. Leonard, D.D., U.S.*

1117 The speaker is evidently a special attendant on Xouthos, for he is a warmer
partizan of him and Iôn, than of Kreousa.

1118 When a murder or suicide takes place in a Christian church, a renewed conse-
cration thereof is necessary.

1120 See 687, 756, 750, 857.

1125 Xouthos' expedition prevents his reappearance on the stage, where his presence
in the ensuing scenes would be inconvenient.

1126 " Dionusos had a temple at Parnassus, no traces of which are now discernible."
*Dodwell.* The Nauplian peak was sacred to Bakkhos, and sacrifices were
offered to him at Parnassus. *Catullus,* 64. 390.

1128 "Take thee a young calf for a sin offering, a calf of the first year, without blemish, for a burnt offering to sacrifice before the Lord." *Levit.* 9. "Armenian and Abyssinian Christian priests still sacrifice beasts upon their altars." *Picart, Chr. Gr.* "The priest censeth the holy gift thrice, saying, Deal favourably with us, O Lord, then wilt thou accept the sacrifice of righteousness, oblations and holocausts, then will they place young calves upon thy altars." *Div. Lit. St. Chrysos.*

1130 The materials being in the temple repositories, and suitable locality in its grounds, a booth, such as here described, might have been erected by sufficient and competent hands in two hours.

1131 Hèra, Artemis, Aphroditè, Eileithuia, Genitulla, and Pan. In its numerous temples Parnassos has been surpassed by Mount Athos, which is 150 miles in circumference, and, in addition to its college of St. Basilius, whence emanates the Greek Christian priesthood, boasts 900 churches and monasteries, whose wealth, accumulated through centuries from pilgrims' gifts, excites the wonder of travellers. See *Murray's Hand-book, Greece.*

1132 So Paley interprets "semnôs." "The Hieros performed many sacerdotal rites." *Pausanias.*

1133 Plethron was a measure of 100 ft. Greek, in length.

1134 He superintended the workmen at their labours. For convenience's sake, some lines in the text are here transposed.

1136 Iôn's friends in the temple and comrades at the college, 663. 1131. In a booth 100 ft. square, allowing for passages and spaces, 336 persons can be seated at tables. "The ancient Greeks did not recline at banquets." *Potter* and *Athen. Deip.* 86. *c.* 20.

1141 In a Spanish bull-ring, "Plaza de los toros," an awning, "el sombrajo," is stretched over that portion of the area on which the sunbeams fall.

1142 Iôn, as sacristan, had control over the temple's contents, 5. 4. See account of the Jewish tabernacles, *Exod.* 25. 28, and of the tent-feast of Ptolomy Philadelphus *Athen. Deip. B.* 5. *c.* 27, also *Esther* 1.

1144 "Herakles, in his boyhood, when novice at Apollo's sanctuary, filled the office of Daphnephoros." *Smith, C. D.*

1147 On a compartment of Achilles' shield a similar design is described in the *Iliad of Homer*, also in *Eurip. Electra.* " The state robes of the Plantagenet Kings were embroidered and overlaid with silver plates, to represent the constellations." *Planche's Costumes.*

151 With yoke and chariot unconnected. The horses of Deities were supposed to precede, but not draw their cars.

154 By an optical illusion, the " Great Bear," preceded and followed by other stars, appears to turn round the polar star, from east to west. Of this constellation, figured as " Charles's wain," the waggon seems to retrograde.

156 " The full moon was rising from the horizon, just as the westering sun was sinking on the opposite side." *Paley.*

157 Phosphoros and Hesperos, the evening and morning star, identical with the planet Venus.

159 Tyrian or Assyrian needlework, of coloured silks and gold and silver thread, such as is now imported from the far east.

161 Human-headed bulls and lions, such as are represented on the slabs exhumed from Ninevch and Babylon.

163 Cecrops is figured, on sculptures and gems, with the lower half of his body formed of serpents.

166 Sewer, in the text, Kêrûx, herald. " The heralds at sacrificial feasts were cooks, and their office was held in high honour." *Clidemus cited by Athenæus,* B. 10. c. 26. Even in the last century, a German elector filled the office of sewer to the emperor.

171 Domestics, in large households, offer to the chief attendant on a distinguished guest the post of honour amongst themselves. Kreousa's favoured slave and Iôn's servant, 1183, acting as head waiter, is so preoccupied with his murderous design, that he makes blunders in the table-service. The text says " he stood in the midst of the plain," hibernicè, " took the floor," anglicè, " took the lead."

174 See note 1187.

175 " Gold cups were nearly unknown in Greece, until the plunder of the Delphic temple by the Phocians, when the precious metals became comparatively abundant." *Athen. Deip. B.* 6. *c.* 20. At the high table only, we may presume.

1176 As Hephaistos is ridiculed, in the Iliad, for assuming the office of Ganumedes, so is the Presbus, here, for claiming that of the young oinouchoi.

1177 At the conclusion of a banquet, hymns were sung to the Gods, in unison with pipes. See note 1194.

1178 "After meals, pure wine was drunk by all in a pledge-cup, and a libation made to the good Genius." *Athen. B.* 15 *c.* 48. We are here reminded of the mediæval "wassail bowl," and the "loving cup," which, at Guildhall, is circulated after a flourish from the silver trumpets; also of the use of a common chalice, at the administration of the holy sacrament, in an Anglican church. "With difficulty I obtained the privilege of drinking out of my own glass, instead of the 'Kulix philotesia,' poculum amicitiæ, which served for the whole party." *Dodwell's Greece,* 1. 157.

1187 "Each uttered a God's name at libations, and spilt some of the liquor, before drinking." *Potter.* "The priest shall offer his drink offering" (vulgate, libatio). *Numbers* 6. "The drink offering shall be of wine." *Levit.* 23. The libation was a minor sacrifice. All washed hands before performing a sacrifice. "And he set the laver between the tent of the congregation, and the altar, . . . . and Moses and Aaron, and their sons, washed hands." *Exod.* 40. 31. 32. "Le boute-hors de table, que l'on servait, lorsque les convives, après s'être lavé les mains, et avoir dit les grâces, &c." *Service au quatorzième siècle, Moyen âge, Lacroix.* "In the Catholic Church, before consecrating the oblation, the priest washes his fingers." *Ordinary of the Mass.* "The Mingrelian Christians, styled the 'orthodox,' still make libations at feasts. The President rises, elevates a filled goblet of wine, and having called upon the name of the Lord God, and saluted the guests, spills half of its contents." *Picart, Gr. Chr.* For an account of the annual libation of the "Gerbe," in France, see *Claudet, Georges Sand.*

1189 Perhaps the servant had dropped a pitcher.

1191 See note 101.

1193 "Had it been a libation, he would have spilt the wine on the table, not upon the ground." *Boethe.* "Statues (statuettes ?) of the Gods were on the board." *Potter, G. A.*

1194 See *Virg. En.* 1. 730. At feasts, before sacrifice, the crier enjoined "silence," and the priests entoned "Let us pray." *Potter.* At Guildhall, the crier, toast-master, calls "Silence for grace," and the canticle of "Non nobis Domine" is sung. Wine, as a beverage of the Greeks, was always mixed with water. Had not this feast been interrupted, the second libation of wine and water would have been made to "Zeus the Saviour," hymns would have been sung, and Iôn, in a speech, would have bid farewell to his comrades. 664.

195 To avert the evil omen, Iôn had sent to the temple for more vessels, and the wine of the Biblinan hills in Thrace, one of the five "grands vins" of Greece. *Hesiod. E.* I. 284.

197 Diodorus relates, lib. 7, that doves were often to be seen at temples. Probably, Augurs made use of them. At St. Mark's, Venice, pigeons, bred and fed at the public cost, are held in reverence, for, to kill them is deemed sacrilege. They never fly beyond the purlieus of the Uffizi. "Though alluded to in the earliest histories of the town, no rational explanation of their presence has been offered." *Murray, H. B. N. I.*

198 Startled, perhaps, by a bird of prey in the hieros' absence. 106.

200 Here is an indication of spring-time and the Delphic festival. The dove, "columba palumba," at pairing and moulting seasons, is subject to cramps and fevers exciting thirst; "when it drinks, it dips its head into the water, and imbibes at one draught, unlike the other 'gallinacea,' who raise their beaks at each sip." *Le Maout. Oiseaux.* All who have kept this bird will testify to its readiness, at spring-time, to absorb wine, and even spirits, and to the benefit which it receives therefrom.

209 Iôn wore the chlamys of an Ephêbos, fastened on the shoulder by a brooch; on this occasion, a heavy embroidered garment which impeded his movements. Royal personages' state robes remain on their thrones during an address therefrom. "The state robes of the Plantagenet Kings were fastened on their shoulders by jewelled clasps." *Planché's Costume.*

214 Questioned, here, means tortured. "In criminal cases evidence of slaves was admissible, only, under torture." *Potter.* "Mettre à la question, to examine under torture." *Fr. Dict.* "Question, examination by torture." *Blackstone.*

219 The Puthion magistrates were the "members of the Amphictyonic Council, who, bound to protect the interests of the Delphic temple, met, annually, in the spring." *Smith, C. D.* The tribunal of the "Ruota," at the Vatican, now, seems to be a somewhat similar court.

1220 "Criminal accusations had to be made on oath." *Potter.* Iôn lays his indictment against Kreousa, in the Amphictyonic hall, calling to witness the ancient Deity Gaia, whose statue stood there, as did those of her cotemporaries, Hestia in the Hellenic Prytaneïa, and Themis in the Roman Tribunes, and as, now, the Crucifix stands in the French Palais de Justice, all for the purpose of attestation. The image of Gaia was in the Delphic hall, because she had uttered oracles there, before Apollo had slain the Python, and established his cult at Parnassus. See *Eum. Æsch.* 2.

1223 "At Delphi was a rock, called Huampse or Hyampeia, from which all guilty of sacrilege were hurled, and their bodies left unburied." *Potter from Lucian.*

1225 Hieros signifies elliptically, but emphatically, one consecrated to a God. See note 55. The term, translated from Holy Scripture as "the holy one," is, in Greek, "ton hagion," and "ton hosion," but nowhere "ton hieron."

1229 Thanatos, the Deity of Death, had neither temples nor priests, nor were prayers offered to him.

1237 "If I take the wings of the morning, and dwell in the uttermost parts of the sea," &c. *Psalm* 129. "Optâ ardua pennis astra sequi, clausumve cavâ te condere terrâ." *En.* 12. 892.

1240 Atê is alluded to, here, as the agent of Destruction.

1244 "In the time of trouble he shall hide me." *Psalm* 27.

1250 Kreousa addresses her two Prospoloi, who have joined the Chorus in the Orchestra, since l. 807; see note, 154.

1255 "Criminals, who reached the Delphic sanctuary, were under the protection of its God, while they remained on his altar steps. Food and necessaries were supplied to them, until they could be safely housed in the temple precincts, from which their escape was facilitated." *Potter, G. A.*

1260 "Their blood, therefore, shall return on the head of Joab." *Kings* 1. 33. *Sam.* 21. 17. *Exod.* 19. 10 Had the guards slain Kreousa in the temple-courts, her punishment would have been theirs, her blood would have been on their heads as well as their own, and the God would have visited the city with some calamity.

1261 The maternal grandfather of Kreousa is addressed by the name of the river into which he was transformed. A river God was styled "Tauromorphous," bull shaped, the rush of a torrent being compared to that of an enraged bull.

We speak of "Father Thames," and "*der vater Rhein;*" also of an obstinate man as "bull-headed," and one who has his own way we liken to a "bull in a china-shop."

A statute of Cephisos stood in the Parthenon's western pediment.

1280 Kreousa had previously insulted the altar and its God. 384.

1283 Kreousa, in terror, appealing to her celestial ravisher for protection, is confident that he will slay whoever assaults her.

1284 The "questioner" is "in common." Some suppose a *double entente* here.

1285 The word "hieros" is played upon in its double sense. Kreousa is sacred to the God, as protected by his sanctuary, and consecrated to him, as victim to his lust.

1286 Iôn uses the word "hieros" in reference to himself. 1225.

1287 See 311.

1290 Two meanings of the word "pious" are here. Iôn uses it to signify one who reverences the Gods, Kreousa one who is free from crime. She endeavours to justify herself.

1293 By "firing Erectheus' house" Kreousa means usurping the throne, and excluding that king's successors. She thinks on her lost son. Iôn understands the word "fire" in its literal sense.

1297 Xouthos, as an alien, could not speak in public. See note, 674.

We are here reminded that neither the late Prince Consort in England, nor the King Consorts in Spain and Portugal, had seats at Cabinet-council-boards.

1298 See Eur. Supp. 108.

1299 "A mercenary had neither vote nor voice in the State, nor could he possess landed property therein." *Potter.*

1301 See 897. Kreousa repeats Presbus' words.

1302 "Envy, not fear, prompted thee to slay me!" To which Kreousa angrily retorts, for the taunt is bitter.

1305 "A natural son could inherit, only, a small portion of his father's property, the bulk of which went to his nearest of kin." *Potter.* Kreousa, having called Xouthos a "hired ally," intimates now that he was paid in money for his services. This ungrateful speech rouses Iôn's indignation.

16

1306 "The afflatus of the God inspired the prophetess." *Potter.* See *Dion Cassius* 13. 62. *Lucian B. 3. Dodwell's Greece,* 1. 179.

1307 "Thy mother exposed thee to death, without reason; I sought thy life in self-defence." Kreousa unwittingly condemns herself. 317.

1310 "The altars, ceiling, columns and images, in the interior of the Delphic temple, were decorated with laurel festoons." *Smith, C. D.*

1311 Apollo would not be pleased, were his temple desecrated by the slaughter of her whom he has ravished.

1312 For reasons offered in note 429, this speech is not given to Iôn here, as it is in all editions.

1316 See Rae Wilson's observations on the "Assassins' Sanctuary at Naples," in his time. *Travels,* 1835 A.D.

1317 The poet foreshadows the establishment of mediæval monasteries.

1329 See 1025, and note.

1333 At Naples is published, annually, a list of possible fortuitous coincidences, which are announced as presaging good and bad luck to those in whose presence they may occur. Influenced by this almanack, the inhabitants of that town purchase lottery tickets, or refrain from doing so.

1335 Puthia's words verify the statement of Pausanias as to the plenary power of the Hieros in the temple.

1338 "Consecrated articles were decorated with tufts of coloured wool." *Potter.* The cradle of the King of Rome, Reichstadt, at the Louvre, is ornamented with gilt garlands and festoons.

1357 See 48.

1375 The "Daimôn genethlion" was a Genius, appointed by Anangkê to attend to the lot, good or bad, of each human being, from life to death. *Pindar, in Puthia,* speaks of "the attendant Daimôn." See *Hom. Od. B.* 14, and *Hesiod E.* 173, and *Greverus' note thereon.* Roman Catholics believe that they are watched, individually, by guardian angels, of whose names and qualities they are not cognizant. See "Litany of the Angel Guardian," "*Golden Manual.*" "Feast of our holy guardian angels, October," *Roman Missal.* "St. Michael and all angels, Sept. 29." *Ang. Ch. Com. Pr. Exod.* 23. 20. "The household Dæmôn of the Boyard of Wallachia." *Anastasius, Hope v. 2.*

1388 " In vain he flees whose destiny pursues him." *Witch of Edmonton. Rowley.*

1411 Here is a play upon a word. Iôn says, " I shall *catch* you out in your tricks."
Kreousa answers, " I wish you would *catch* me in your arms !"

1421 Theocritus, in his Idylls, alludes to Athenian infants wrapped in Gorgon-
embroidered cloths.

1427 Badham's emendation of "sarkazontes" is here accepted. Gold-snake
bracelets, with carbuncle eyes, in facsimile of Erectheus' belt, are here
alluded to.

1428 Iôn questions Kreousa as to the form of the ornament which she describes.
The translator has rearranged some lines which he believes to have been
erroneously transposed in the MSS.

1429 A gipsy woman clasps her hereditary collar of beads round the neck of her
newly-born infant. *Like and Unlike. Braddon.*

1433 At the contest of Poseidon and Pallas for the patronage of Cecrops' capital, the
former produced a fountain, and the latter an olive-tree. This plant, being
evergreen, was supposed to be immortal. Perhaps the sculptures on the
Parthenon's tympanum are here alluded to. As " Poseidon struck the rock
with his trident, and the water gushed forth," so " Moses struck the rock with
his rod (divining rod) thrice, and the waters flowed abundantly." *Numbers 20.*
" The original olive-tree created by Pallas, was said to be in the temple courts
of Pandrosus, at Athens." *Williams' Views in Greece.*

1439 " O Luce magis dilecta." *En.* 4. 31. In Italian and Spanish is the same
expression, " O Luce d'anima mia !" " O Luz de mi alma !"

1442 On the Artemisian drum, at the British Museum, is a sculptured group, representing Persephonê receiving the shade of a veiled female, conducted by Hermes
and Thanatos.

1444 Iôn alludes to one of those redeemed from death by Esculapius.

1456 " As him seemeth best, let him dispose !
Enjoy thou what he gives to thee !" *Milton, Par. L.*

1459 Compare line 959.

1464 " Behold thy king cometh unto thee !" *Zach.* 9. 9.

1465 " There shall come a rod out of the stem of Jesse." *Isaiah* 11. 1.

1466 " The people that walked in darkness have seen a great light . . . and upon them hath the light shined." " Arise, shine, for the light is come! The days of thy mourning shall be ended." *Isaiah* 9. 4. 6. 10.

1467 By the word " Helios " is there a concetto, alluding to Iôn as Phoibos' son?

1468 The predicament in which she stands suddenly occurs to Kreousa, in the midst of her exultation. Iôn imagines himself to be the son of Xouthos and Kreousa, and that he was educated at Delphi, for some reasons, without his father's and mother's knowledge.

1474 The nuptial procession to a bridegroom's house was accompanied by guests bearing torches, and professional singers and dancers. *Potter.* For a similar passage see *Pindar, Puth. c.* 3. *E.* 1, where reference is made to Coronis. The same marriage ceremonies are observed now amongst the Coptic Christians. *Picart.* These rhymes stand as in the original text. The metre, doubtless, intended to suggest a wedding dance, recalls, exactly, the movement of the " Air des lampions," so popular in France.

1477 A form of adjuration. Gorgophona, Gorgonicide, was a name of Pallas. See note 991. She was also called Gorgophora. *Lempriere.* Olives, see 1433.

1482 Nightingales, in temple gardens, are alluded to in *Æd. Col. Soph.* 18.

1484 Kreousa is, properly, silent to her son on the circumstance of her rape, which she had communicated to her waiting women, 895, and her old slave, 941.

1487 Greeks and Latins reckoned by lunar months, "Decumâ mense nascetur puer." *Amph. Plaut.*

1490 She knew that her mother, Praxithea, would, like everyone else, discredit her story of her adventure with the God. 898.

1493 The law enjoined that new-born children should be bathed. *Callimachus.*

1501 From this line may we presume that sons could not prosecute their parents in law-courts? Iôn reflects that his mother has twice, deliberately, perilled his life. Not yet having been dispensed from his sacred office, he exercises his plenary powers in the temple, and annuls Kreousa's sentence.

1514 Tukhe, the deity of good and evil fortune, was a handmaid to the Moirai, the fates, who, " in some of the Greek Islands, are still worshipped with superstitious rites." *Anastas. Hope,* c. 11. 150. A statue of Tukhê stood in the Parthenon's eastern pediment.

1516 " To know that which before us lies, in daily life, is the true wisdom." *Milton, P. L.*

1535 " By Attic law, any man may assume the family name of a freeman who has adopted him as heir." *Potter.*

1537 " Falsehood is incompatible with Deity." *Calderon de la Barca.*

1541 Aristophanes, in his *Ornithes*, quotes the law of Solon on a similar case, and ridicules this very passage.

1550 The presence of Deities was notified by peals of thunder and flashes of light. *Phædrus* 5. 7. *Amphi. Plaut.* 5. *Exodus* 16. 19. *Acts* 9. 3.

1551 The sight of a Deity, in person, was supposed to be the precursor of death. " Thou canst not see my face, for thou shalt not see me and live." *Exod.* 33. " We shall surely die, because we have seen God." *Judges* 13. " We are about to receive the king of all, before the holy communion, who cometh invisibly." *Div. Lit. St. Chrysos.* The Gods, in the Iliad, present themselves in the shapes of human beings. " Jupiter, ita, se versipellem facit quando lubet." *Amph. Plaut.* " Then he appeared in another form." *Mark* 16. 12.

1552 " And is he gone, mine Absolom ?-
Then shall he behold his Sov'reign face to face !" *Peele's David.*

1553 " Ne time! Et tibi et tuis propitius, cœli cultor advenit! Nihil est quod timeas!" *Amph. Plaut. A.* 5. " And the angel said unto her, fear not." *Luke* 1. *John* 12. 28.

" Aussitôt parut une dame
dont l'aspect émut notre cœur,
mais elle rassura notre âme,
en nous disant, n'ayez pas peur ! "

*Refrain. Solennité anniversaire de l'apparition de la T. S. Vierge à la Salette. Manuel des pèlerins.* 12°. *Paris,* A.D. 1886.

1557 Can these two lines be genuine? They seem admissible only in a burlesque! Has some mischievous wag foisted them in? The earliest extant MS. of the play is of the fourteenth century only.

1563 All in the temple and its precincts. See 1218.

1565 " By secondary means," viz. the doves and the cradle.

1570 Yoked the horses *for*, not *to*, the car. See 1151 and note.

1576 By " root unique " meaning " by the same father and mother."

1579 Some have supposed that the different castes of a nascent colony are here alluded to, viz. the priestly, military, trading, and agricultural.

1585 On both sides of the Hellespont.

1587 "Apollo was the patron of the Gentiles in Ionia." *Chambers's Miscell. G. R.*

1588 Ionia was thus named before the birth of Iôn.

1594 Achaios, here mentioned, could not have founded, nor could he have given his name to, Achaia, of which so styled country his father was a native. 63.

1595 "Dieu fait bien les choses, quand il s'y met." *Pontalec, Dennery*. Phoibos, as Paian, patron of the healing art, averted from Kreousa the maladies attending child-birth. *Il bambino dell' Ara Cæli*, at Rome, is believed to assume the same benevolent office, for its image is introduced, by priests in procession, into the chambers of women in travail. See *Pictures of Italy, C. Dickens.*

1596 14. 340.

1602 Let Xouthos continue to believe that he is Iôn's father!

1604 "Behold, I bring you good tidings of great joy." *Luke 2. 9.*

1606 The pious Delphic pupil bows to what he believes to be divine revelation, and implicitly credits what he has hitherto deemed blasphemous to allude to. 339. 429. 1524.

1608 Kreousa's story of her adventure with Phoibos, though she had sworn to it, Iôn could not believe, persuaded that she had invented it to conceal the shame of her seduction by some humble swain. 341. 1525. 1531. Nothing short of celestial interference can overcome the hieros' religious scruples. As here is a "dignus vindice nodus,"
     "The thunder roars and Pallas' car descends."

1613 See 249. For "roptra" see 108 and note.

1616 Kreousa appears heartless, in proceeding to Athens without Xouthos, of whose innocence she is aware, and taking with her him whom he believes to be his son; but she is bound to obey the commands of Pallas, who has expressed her intention, as patroness of her town, of accompanying her. In the Odyssey Pallas is represented as not following, but preceding, Telemachus on his journey.

1618 Kreousa now has a son to succeed her. 268.

1620 With moral reflections upon the scenes and characters of his creation, the poet concludes his song. The first of these lines refers to the impatience under calamity, and the impiety, of Kreousa; the third to her happy conversion, her repentance, and gratitude to Heaven; and the second to the purity and piety of Iôn, who is duly rewarded.

" Trust in the Lord, and wait patiently for him! Mark the perfect man, and behold the upright, for the end of that man is peace; but the transgressors shall be destroyed together; the end of the wicked shall be cut off." *Psalm* 37.

" Si l'homme fait le bien, son âme, dégagée de son corps par la mort, sera absorbée dans l'essence divine, et ne ranimera plus un corps de terre. Mais l'âme du méchant restera revêtue des quatre éléments; et après qu'elles (les âmes ?) auront été punies, elles reprendront un corps; mais, si elles ne reprennent leur première pureté, elles ne seront jamais absorbées dans le sein de BRAHM." *Le Narud, traduit par Holwell.*

THE END.